COUNSELING
AND
SPIRITUALITY:

Christian Biblical Principles
Within Daily Meditations/Reflections
For The Journey/Adventure

Dr. Jerry Kiser

Dr. Tommy Turner

Dr. Marvin Jenkins

Sleepytown Press
Anniston, Alabama

Counseling and Spirituality
Translations Of The Bible Utilized Throughout The Book

ISBN: 978-1-937269-94-1

Sleepy Town Press
1436 Nocoseka Trail
Suite 0-4
Anniston, Alabama 36207

E-mail: sleepytownpress@gmail.com

www.sleepytownpress.com

Photographs of Churches by Jerry Kiser
Photographs of The Lamb, The Lion, and The Knight by Jerry Kiser
Art Work: The Lamb, The Lion, and the Knight © Jerry Kiser 2010

Artwork: Created by Jerry Kiser and Jason Wright

DEDICATION

In memory of the twenty-six individuals who came together in July 1913 and founded Ivy Memorial Baptist Church:

Joel O. Adams	J. T. Gay	L. B. Saunders
Mrs. L. F. Beazlie	Mrs. J. T. Gay	Mrs. L. B. Saunders
Miss Annie Beazlie	Maylan H. Gay	Fred Shawen
Mill Lalla Beazlie	G. B. King	Warren Smith
O. J. Brittingham	C. F. Hartman	Mrs. Warren Smith
Mrs. Mary Burrell	Mrs. C. F. Hartman	Miss Abbie Smith
Mrs. C. W. Cooper	Mrs. T. B. Kyle	Clark B. Smith
Miss Ruth Cooper	C. B. Saunders	J. T. Temple
Mrs. J. H. Ellis	Mrs. C. B. Saunders	

I am praying not only for these disciples, but also for all who will ever believe in Me (Jesus) through their message.

John 17:20 (NLT)

TABLE OF CONTENTS

PROLOGUE

The date was Friday, February 5, 2010. My plan was a two-hour airplane trip home. However, a weather front cancelled several air flights – one of which was mine. Due to some work responsibilities, other travel alternatives had to be considered – and I decided to drive from Virginia to Alabama. A two-hour air travel trip became a twelve-hour automobile trip.

The twelve-hour road trip provided me with some unexpected time alone with God. The twelve hours were spent praying, listening to Christian music, and listening to Christian talk radio. By the time I reached Alabama, I thought I had a sermon outline.

As I began to read scriptures in an attempt to fill in the sermon outline, the sermon outline became a deck of one hundred forty (three by five) note cards. These note cards reflected some of the principles of God that help guide and assist in living the Christian life – both the joys and challenges of the journey/adventure.

These note cards have now become the manuscript that you hold in your hands. My plan was a two-hour airplane trip. Knowing "all things work together for good to them that love God, to them who are called according to His purpose" (Romans 8:28, KJV), and accepting the cancellation of air travel – well that allowed God to show up in a most unexpected and unplanned way. Including God in the journey turns the journey into an adventure. Air travel, that turned into a road trip, that turned into an outline, that turned into note cards, that turned into a three year writing labor of love, and that finally turned into this book. All these turnings demonstrate the wonder of God!

INTRODUCTION

If you have picked up this book and are now reading these words, we hope that the title has sparked some interest in you concerning the counsel of God in regard to spiritual/ psychological principles that can be discovered through personal meditations/reflections that will assist you and equip you for the journey/adventure of life. The age old questions involving the meaning of life, the purpose of life, and the spiritual/psychological principles of how to live an effective life are worth pursuing. If awareness and insight regarding these questions is gained and woven into the tapestry of one's life, then the cycle of life (which includes death) involving both joys and sorrows, positives and negatives, and gains as well as losses become easier to embrace.

The authors of this book are professional counselors with a combined total of over 100 years counseling experience, and are all Christians with a combined total of over 120 years of learning to grow/develop in the love and grace of God. Andy Andrews believes "...experience is not the best teacher. Other people's experience is the best teacher" (2009, *The Noticer*, page 9). With that in mind, the authors have chosen to share what their experiences have taught them.

In the Lifespan Development course that I teach, I often ask my graduate students, "If you could go back in time to the age of 18 and live your life again, would you?" Very few students raise their hand. However, when I ask the same question with a slight modification, "If you could go back in time to the age of 18 WITH WHAT YOU NOW KNOW, and live your life over again, would you?", the majority of students raise their hand. This change in response pattern indicates that there is something of great value that is acquired through life experience.

Samuel Gladding defines counseling as the "process in which clients learn how to make decisions and formulate new ways of behaving, feeling, and thinking… counseling involves both choice and change" (1996, Counseling: A Comprehensive Profession, page 8). The multitude of decisions that we make daily represents choice. That change is part of living is clearly evidenced by the passage of time, the changing of the seasons, and the aging of the individual.

In Isaiah 9:6 (KJV) we find that one of the names of Jesus is "wonderful counselor." In John 1:1(KJV) and Revelation 19:13(KJV), Jesus is referred to as the "Word of God." In Psalm 119:105 (KJV) we learn "Your Word is a lamp unto my feet and a light to my path." These scriptures indicate that Jesus can serve as our counselor through the written Word of God and provide light to our path in the journey/adventure of life.

While discussing the concepts of counseling and spirituality, Joshua Gold provides a glimpse into the meaning of spirituality through the sharing of the following words: "connotes a direct personal experience of the sacred…and of one's search for meaning and belonging and the core values that influence one's behavior" (2010, Counseling and Spirituality: Integrating Spiritual and Clinical Orientations, page 6). The key words that I want to highlight are a "personal experience of the sacred that influences one's behavior." I would like to suggest that this personal experience of the sacred can also influence one's feelings, thoughts, and choices – thus influence the process of change by utilizing the individual's personal experience of the sacred as part of the counseling process to influence one's behaviors, feelings, thoughts, and choices. Uniting counseling with spirituality will provide a more wholistic approach to working with clients. Seeking out and including spiritual principles contained within the various sacred writings that are specific to the client's approach to spirituality will serve to assist in the counseling process. This more wholistic approach to counseling will facilitate client awareness/insight into the meaning of life, the purpose of life, and the spiritual/psychological principles of how to live an effective life. This is true not only for counseling clients, but also for individuals seeking to include spirituality as part of the process of life --- the joys, the challenges, as well as the changes that are a natural part of the journey/adventure.

W. E Vine defines the word mediate as "be diligent in, to attend to, and to practice" (1940, An Expository Dictionary of New Testament Words, page 55). Joyce Meyer shares that the word meditate means "to roll over and over in your mind...to mutter, converse aloud with oneself, or declare something" (2012,Change Your Words: Change Your Life, page 62). The Word of God tells us "his delight and desire are in the law of the Lord, and on His law (the precepts, the instructions, the teachings of God) he habitually meditates (ponders and studies) by day and by night" (Psalm 1:2, AMP). Knowing God and the Word of God are prerequisites to having God provide the light that illuminates our path in the journey/adventure of life.

Webster's New World Dictionary (2003) defines the word reflection as "contemplation." Emmaus Ministries of Silicon Valley provides insight into contemplation by sharing the following words: "A long loving look at the real...contemplative prayer attempts to shift us more toward the listening...to engage us relationally and emotively with God. Meditation is its counterpart that seeks to engage us mentally and cognitively with God" (www. authenticdiscipleship.org; Contemplating God in Scripture; Date Accessed November 10, 2012). In John 1:12 (AMP) we are told "to as many as did receive and welcome Him, He gave the authority [power, privilege, right] to become the children of God." In Matthew 6:9 (AMP) we are told to "Pray, therefore like this: Our Father." These words serve to remind us that we are in relationship with God. God is our Father, and we are His children. As we read the Word of God, we need to seek God not only mentally and cognitively, but also seek God emotively and relationally.

The Webster's New World Dictionary (2003) defines journey as traveling from one place to another, and adventure as a daring, hazardous undertaking. In First Peter 2:11 (NKJV) we read, "Beloved, I beg you as sojourners and pilgrims..." – sojourners and pilgrims, words that can help clarify the words journey and adventure.

The Free Dictionary (www.thefreedictionary.com) defines sojourn as a brief period of residence and pilgrim as one who embarks on a quest for something conceived of as sacred, a brief period of residence and a quest for the sacred. Perhaps the best commentary regarding the words journey, adventure, sojourner, and pilgrim can be found in Hebrews 13:14 (NLT), "For this world is not our home, we are looking forward to our city in heaven, which is yet to come," and First Peter 5:8 (NIV), "Be self-controlled and alert. Your enemy, the devil, prowls around like a roaring lion looking for someone to devour."

Additional commentary regarding the words journey, adventure, sojourner, and pilgrim can be found in the writings of Joyce Meyer and C. S. Lewis. In Battlefield of the Mind by Joyce Meyer we read, "We are engaged in a war. Our enemy is Satan. The mind is the battlefield" (1995, page 16). C. S. Lewis shares very similar thoughts when he writes, "Enemy occupied territory – that is what the world is...I must keep alive in myself the desire for my true country, which I shall not find till after death; I must never let it get snowed under or turned aside; I must make it the main object of life to press on to that other country and to help others to do the same." (1952, Mere Christianity, page 46 and page 137)

The introduction, up to this point, has sought to establish a relationship between the words contained within the title and the words that will be found throughout the manuscript. Contained throughout the book, the reader will also see photographs of churches and photographs of the painting "The Lamb, The Lion, And The Knight". The painting serves to remind us of the Love and Power of God and that we are part of the Army of God here on earth. These photographs of churches are the visible sign or symbol of the fact that God dwells among us, with the church serving as the epicenter through which the gospel (the good news) of God's Love and Provision for Salvation and Redemption flow as a result of the work of God's Army throughout the world. As C.S. Lewis explains, "When you go to church you are really listening into the secret wireless from our friends; that is why the enemy is so anxious to prevent us from going" (1952, Mere Christianity, page 46).

Many of these congregations have chosen to include a cross as part of the church building structure. The cross is the symbol of the atoning work that Jesus completed at Calvary. The cross is there to evoke a multitude of thoughts, feelings, and memories. Seeing the cross may cause an individual to reflect on Sundays of yesteryear and the singing of hymns that brought peace, joy, comfort, hope, and faith. The words of the hymn, "At the Cross" are an excellent example:

At the cross, at the cross

Where I first saw the light,

And the burden of my heart rolled away,

It was there by faith

I received my sight

(Baptist Hymnal, 1956, edited by Walter Hines Sims, At the Cross, by Isaac Watts and Ralph Hudson).

The words of the hymn are echoed in John 9:25 (KJV) "I was blind, but now I see." In addition to the words of the hymn and the scripture, C. S. Lewis provides even more clarity when, he writes, "I believe in Christianity as I believe that the sun has risen, not only because I see it, but because by it, I see everything else."

(2002, Essay Collection: Faith, Christianity, and the Church, page 21, [Edited by Lesley Walmsley]).

Hopefully the photographs of churches, the photographs of the painting, the words of scripture, the words from hymns, the author's words, and the individual's personal meditations/reflections will unite and facilitate the individual's understanding of and the inclusion of God and the eternal as part of the journey/adventure. As C. S. Lewis so eloquently states, "Christianity asserts that every individual human being is going to live forever, and this must be either true or false. Now there are a good many things which would not be worth bothering about if I were going to live only seventy years, but which I had better bother about very seriously if I am going to live forever"

(1952, Mere Christianity, page 74).

HOUSE OF THE LORD

I was glad when they said unto me, Let us go into the house of the Lord! Psalm 122:1(KJV)

The words of Psalm 122 are above the entrance door of this church. As we begin our journey together, let your first step take you into the house of the Lord. Going into God's church is an excellent way to obtain guidance and direction from God as you seek to navigate the journey of life. Ask God for wisdom and insight regarding the purpose of your life.

Seek ye first the Kingdom of God and His righteousness and all these things shall be added unto you (Matthew 6:33, KJV). C. S. Lewis echoes Matthew 6:33 when he writes, "look for Christ and you will find Him, and with Him everything else thrown in" (1952, Mere Christianity, page 227). You know what your personal "ALL these things" are. As you seek God, may the needed points of navigation be revealed (as you need them) for the decisions of life that will lead you to "ALL these things".

...The book of life of the Lamb that was slain [in sacrifice] from the foundation of the world. Revelation 13:8 (AMP)

In addition to the pictures of churches that serve as a visible symbol that God dwells among us --- this photograph of the painting of The Lamb, The Lion, and The Knight will appear in conjunction with some meditations/reflections to remind us of the love of God as well as the judgment of God. Understanding and insight, into the painting, can be enhanced by meditating and reflecting on the following scriptures:

1) Revelation 5:6 (AMP) And there between the throne and the four living creatures (beings) and among the elders [of the heavenly Sanhedrin] I saw a Lamb standing as though it had been slain...

2) John 1:29 (AMP) The next day John saw Jesus coming to him, and said, Look! There is the Lamb of God Who takes away the sin of the world!

3) Revelation 5:5 (AMP) ...see, the lion of the tribe of Judah, the root (source) of David, has won (has overcome and conquered)! ...

4) Revelation 6:16 (AMP)...hide us from the face of Him Who sits on the throne and from the deep seated indignation and wrath of the Lamb.

5) Revelation 13:8 (AMP) ...everyone whose name has not been recorded in the Book of Life of the Lamb that was slain [in sacrifice] from the foundation of the world.

6) Revelation 12:11 (AMP) And they have overcome (conquered) him [Satan, the devil] by means of the blood of the Lamb and by the utterance of their testimony...

7) Revelation 17:14 (AMP) They will wage war against the Lamb, and the Lamb will triumph over them; for He is Lord of Lords and King of Kings – and those with Him and on His side are chosen and called [elected] and loyal and faithful followers.

8) Colossians 2:15 (AMP) God disarmed the principalities and powers that were ranged against us and made a bold display and public example of them, in triumphing over them in Him and in it [the cross].

9) Ephesians 6:10-20 (AMP) The armor of God (paraphrase) – helmet of salvation, breastplate of righteousness, shield of faith, shoes of the gospel of peace, belt of truth, and the sword of the spirit which is the Word of God.

The Lamb of God represents the love, grace, mercy, and salvation that are available to each one of us as a result of the death of Jesus on the cross at Calvary, the burial of Jesus in the tomb of Joseph of Arimathaea, and the resurrection of Jesus "annulled death and made it of no effect and brought life and immortality" (Second Timothy 1:10, AMP). The Lion of Judah represents the power of God that will be manifested at the point in time when all will come into "...the presence of God and of Christ Jesus, Who is to judge the living and the dead..." (Second Timothy 4:1, AMP) and "that in (at) the name of Jesus every knee should (must) bow, in heaven and on earth and under the earth, and every tongue [frankly and openly] confess and acknowledge that Jesus Christ is Lord, to the glory of God the Father" (Philippians 2:10-11, AMP). The Knight represents the loyal and faithful followers who choose to respond to the love of God and bow their knee to the Lamb of God – thus becoming a member of the army of God who seeks to overcome evil with good (Romans 12:21, KJV).

The painting of the Lamb, the Lion, and the Knight represents the fact that there is both the love of God and the judgment of God. Each, individual, must choose to accept or reject the love of God. Choosing to accept the love of God places you in the army of God and requires that you strive to overcome evil with good, utilizing the tools and power that God provides. According to Dwight L. Moody, "The world has yet to see what almighty God can and will do with, for, through, in, and by a man wholly and fully yielded to Him and to His service" (David Allan Black, 2005, http://covenantnews.com/daveblack050816.htm, Date Accessed 2-2-2013).

What would the world see if God had a whole army of Christian men, women, and children who were "wholly and fully yielded to Him and His service." For now, we can only imagine! (Please review the meditation "Imagine")

CRY TO GOD

Be merciful and gracious to me, O God, ... I will cry to God Most High, ...He will send from heaven and save me from the slanders and reproaches of him who would trample me down or swallow me up, ... Selah [pause, and calmly think of that]! Psalm 57:1-3 (AMP)

Charles Stanley states that, "everyone experiences trials, dangers, heartaches, and doubts. We all face situations where we feel vulnerable, abandoned, and helpless" (2012, Ultimate Conversation, page 66). However, Psalm 57 tells us that when we find ourselves in these experiences and situations that we can cry out to God ---- and God will help us.

Selah, pause and calmly think of that – pause and think about the love and mercy of God that is available to help you face the daily challenges of life. Selah, pause and think. In our fast paced society, it is often difficult to slow down. The Word of God says Selah, pause and think. The Bible also states in Psalm 46:10 (KJV) "Be still and know that I am God." So the question becomes, "will you commit to slowing your life down, and spend time getting to know God, developing your relationship with God?" Selah, pause and think about that. (Note: We pray that as you consider this commitment, that the Holy Spirit will open your eyes and illuminate what you will receive or forfeit based upon your decision.)

BEFORE YOU WERE BORN

Before I formed you in the womb, I knew you; before you were born, I set you apart; I appointed you to be a prophet to the nations.   Jeremiah 1:5 (NIV)

Think of it--- He knew me…and ordained me to be… Before we were even born, the omniscient, omnipotent God of the universe, the Creator of life, knew me! He had a purpose for my life! God told Jeremiah that HE had "ordained" (KJV) him to be a prophet. God had "appointed" (NIV) Jeremiah to be a prophet. The Hebrew word translated "appointed" and "ordained" carries the idea that God had "cut Jeremiah out" to be a prophet. God has "cut you and me out" to be something, somebody special!

Many good, noble people have a benevolent side to them that causes them to want to "help others." While it is a good compulsion, an ever greater motivation is a sense that God has called you --- He has "cut you out"---   to do a specific thing, like counseling.

Great joy comes in the journey of life when we have the settled peace deep within that we are doing what we are "cut out to do"! We will continue to have great joy as we walk in His purpose in every season of life.

BELIEVE AND BE SAVED

They replied, "Believe in the Lord Jesus, and you will be saved – you and your household." Acts 16:31 (NIV)

The setting for this often quoted verse was in a Roman prison where Paul and Silas were jailed. A violent earthquake had just taken place that was strong enough to open all of the doors and loose everyone's chains. The jailer knew the penalty for allowing prisoners to escape would be harsh, and rather than face his superiors, he drew his sword to take his own life. It was at this point that Paul shouted, "Do not harm yourself! We are all here!" (Acts 16:28, NIV). The guard immediately recognized that there was something special about these Christians, and he asked Paul what he needed to do to be saved – and you know the rest of the story.

Salvation is as simple as repenting of your sinful past and accepting Jesus as Lord and Savior. It is a gift from God that cannot be purchased, earned, or gained by good deeds. It comes as an example of pure grace freely given out of love. While it is difficult to understand how this is possible in a world where nothing is really free, God's plan for our salvation is a most precious gift. Jesus paid the price long ago on the cross. The sin debt was paid in full through the sacrifice of the unblemished Lamb. If you do not know Jesus as your Savior, why not make that decision for eternity today?

SET BEFORE YOU LIFE AND DEATH

This day I call heaven and earth as witnesses against you that I have set before you life and death, blessings and curses. Now choose life, so that you and your children may live and that you may love the Lord your God, listen to His voice, and hold fast to Him. For the Lord is your life, and He will give you many years in the land He swore to give your fathers, Abraham, Isaac and Jacob. Deuteronomy 30:19 (NIV)

God did not populate the planet with a humanity designed like robotic creatures. His desire was to enter into a loving fellowship with us through choice as evidenced in the Garden of Eden. But as it turned out, wrong choices have been made from the onset of creation. The tempter lured the first couple into thinking something was missing in their lives. They made a personal choice to disobey God – despite God's clear warning of the consequences. They made a personal choice to fulfill a personal desire so as to fulfill a personal curiosity – and fulfilling that personal desire/curiosity came with a great price tag.

Does this ring true for most of us? Countless times our choices are not need-based, rather they are borne out of a want that has little if anything to do with standing in the will of our Father. God desires to bless us, and He explains in simple language how to claim and enjoy the treasure. We are to love Him, be tuned into His voice and instruction, and finally, to hold fast to Him with rock solid confidence even when our circumstances seem impossible to overcome. The promise God made to Moses and the Israelites is as valid today as it was in those ancient times. Choose life and blessings.

I KNOW GOD

And this is life eternal, that they may know Thee, the only true God, and Jesus Christ, whom Thou has sent. John 17:3 (KJV)

This is the only definition of eternal life in the Bible. The word of Jesus simply and profoundly states that eternal life is knowing God and knowing Jesus.

Carl Jung (http://www.youtube.com/watch?v=WJ25Ai_FYU); Date Accessed November 8, 2012) made a statement that has amazed many and bewildered some: "I do not believe in God; I know God." Whether intended or not, the statement reminds us that a relationship with God is not an academic exercise; it is a personal experience. Eternal life is not acquiring knowledge or giving intellectual assent; it is intimate acquaintance with God.

BOOK OF REMEMBRANCE

Then those who feared the Lord talked often one to another; and the Lord listened and heard it, and a book of remembrance was written before Him of those who reverenced and worshipfully feared the Lord and who thought on His name.   Malachi 3:16 (AMP)

Just as there is a book of remembrance for God regarding "those who reverenced and worshipfully feared the Lord and who thought on His name," each of us can consider keeping a book of remembrance regarding our relationship with God. In Exodus 29:46 (AMP) we are told "they shall know [from personal experience] that I am the Lord their God." This book of remembrance can include our personal experiences with God that strengthened our faith. This book of remembrance will help us to "come boldly unto the throne of grace that we may obtain mercy, and find grace to help in time of need" (Hebrews 4:16, KJV) when we are experiencing spiritual/psychological challenges to our faith that seem overwhelming. In Second Corinthians1:8-9 (AMP) we are told how Paul was so overwhelmed that he "despaired even of life [itself]", however, the purpose of the challenge was to keep him from trusting in and depending on self – but to trust in and depend on God. In Proverbs 3:5- 6(AMP) we are told, "Lean on, trust in, and be confident in the Lord with all your heart and mind and do not rely on your own insight or understanding. In all your ways know, recognize and acknowledge Him, and He will direct and make straight and plain your paths."

Sometimes when we feel overwhelmed, we may not be able to remember the goodness and reality of God. A personal book of remembrance will help us to remember – to remember that the grace of God is available to help us in our time of need, and to remember the times that our confidence in God helped us through a difficult challenge earlier in the journey/adventure.

GRACE FAITH SALVATION

For it is by grace you have been saved, through faith - and this is not from yourselves, it is the gift of God - not by works, so that no one can boast. Ephesians 2:8-9 (NIV)

As one reads the Old Testament, it becomes clear how difficult it was for a Jew to meet the demands of the law under the existing covenant between God and His people. For every breach of the law, much is required to make amends for a given transgression. The people living under the Old Testament were subject to strict rules governing every aspect of their lives. All this changed when Jesus came to live among His people. He came to teach and lead them and ultimately give His life on the cross as the perfect sacrifice to pay the sin-debt once and for all. A new covenant was established as a result of this perfect sacrifice.

Yet even with the freedom extended to us under the new covenant, many Christians labor to be acceptable to the Father. Some go so far as to keep a mental list of the number of times they have attended church, their record of charitable giving, and other self-imposed indicators of being an acceptable child of God. While these aspects of the believer's life should be considered indicators of our love for God, if one is not careful ---a healthy relationship can be turned into an accounting problem.

Ephesians 2:8-9 speaks clearly to the fact that salvation is a gift and that no one can boast, brag about, or earn. God thinks and operates in direct opposition to the worldview where some, kind of, "payback" is expected for most gifts. Are you not glad that Jesus has paid the sin-debt. We cannot gain any more love or acceptability than we already have in our possession. Our acceptability is made possible through Christ alone.

NOW IS THE TIME

As God's fellow workers, we urge you not to receive God's grace in vain. For He says, "In the time of my favor I heard you, and in the day of salvation I helped you." I tell you, now is the time of God's favor, now is the day of salvation. 2 Corinthians 6:1-2 (NIV)

The focus of Paul's ministry was to fulfill the Great Commission. He had a passion for leading people to Christ, both Jew and gentile. As Paul delivers these words of invitation, there is also another message that communicated urgency to those who listened to accept the wonderful, healing gift that Jesus provides for those who accept Him as Lord and Savior.

Do you sense the urgency to make a decision to allow Jesus into your life? We live in times of great uncertainty and anxiety. International tensions around the globe, financial crisis looming on the horizon, severe health issues, and the list goes on. Jesus Christ offers peace and joy to the believer that cannot be otherwise realized. All you have to do is yield to the still, small voice that beckons you to Him. You can experience a new found freedom by making a choice to follow the loving shepherd, Jesus.

If you are a convicted believer, you are privileged to continue carrying out Paul's ministry by your daily witness and testimony. God, through grace, has equipped you perfectly and completely to be effective in issuing the call. It is, indeed, urgent.

NEW MIND – NEW SELF

You were taught with regard to your former way of life, to put off your old self, which is being corrupted by its deceitful desires; to be made new in the attitude of your minds; and to put on the new self, created to be like God in true righteousness and holiness. Ephesians 4:22-24 (NIV)

Whether you are struggling as a new Christian or a seasoned follower of Christ, there is a good likelihood that you face daily challenges in your efforts to subdue the old self. We are creatures of habit and tend to find it difficult to change the way we respond personally to the world around us. The more we try to make significant changes by using our own willpower and determination, the more we are frustrated and demoralized by our failure to achieve the result God seeks from us.

Ephesians 4:22-24 shows us how to become the new creature that God has made possible through our salvation, the first step in a follower's life. We then need to focus on renewing our mind by regularly reading God's word and establishing a disciplined prayer life. This activity opens up the channels of communication between us and the Creator. The more we read, pray, and meditate --- the more we will become like Him. Having fellowship with other Christians can also be helpful. It is the power of His grace that makes change possible. Join Jesus at the table daily and you will experience new power and vitality in your life.

GOD IS WITH YOU

Be strong and of good courage; be not afraid, neither be dismayed; for the Lord thy God is with thee, wherever you go. Joshua 1:9 (KJV)

Courage is more easily seen than it is defined: a ten-year-old swallows hard and stands in front of the class and recites the assigned poem; a sheepish young adolescent boy asks the class beauty for a date; a worker confronts a co-worker when inappropriate actions call for a challenge; a black woman refuses to give up her seat and go to the back of the bus at the demand of a white man; Polycarp, a devout Christian, refuses to recant when facing being burned at the stake for his religion. Courage can be seen in each and all of these examples. It is notable that, in each instance, courage is shown by the individuals independently, solitarily, apparently alone.

It is easier to muster courage in a group. The "esprit de corps," the team spirit, group motivation, can create more of a "lynch mob" exhilaration that spurs the group to action. Is that really courage? Might not courage at its finest be defined as personal, individual resolve to act – alone if necessary -- out of some deeply held principle, value, or devotion, regardless of consequence?

And yet, the word of the Lord that came to Joshua assures that we are not alone! The omnipotent God is with us at all times! God's later promise to and through Isaiah (41:10, KJV) echoed the promise to Joshua, and gave rise to the hymn that has inspired courage in millions:

"Fear not, I am with thee

Oh be not dismayed;

For I am thy God

And will still give thee aid.

I'll strengthen thee, help thee,

And cause thee to stand,

Upheld by my righteous,

Omnipotent hand." (Baptist Hymnal, 1956, Edited By Walter Hines Sims, How Firm A Foundation, By John Rippon)

In the journey of life, circumstances calling for courageous action will arise. You must act-- you will act-- from what appears to be independent resolve. But you will know that you are not alone; God is with you, supplying His eternal strength. Be strong!

MERCY FOR SINNERS

God be merciful to me a sinner. Luke 18:13 (KJV)

The ability to show unconditional positive regard for others is a cardinal virtue of successful counselors. Counselors are to view others – and treat others--- as deserving of respect. Others are viewed as people of infinite, eternal worth and value. There is no room for condescension; there is no room for a "holier-than-thou" attitude. There is no place for despising others who may have made mistakes we have not made, who may not measure up to our standards.

Jesus gave the parable of the praying Pharisee and tax collector, which provides the context for the verse above, to portray how self-righteous persons despise others. The Pharisee, obsessively concerned with comparing himself to others, called God's attention to the fact that he was not evil and sinful like the tax collector. He then picked out a few virtues to extol before God. Yes, he "tooted his own horn"!

In sharp contrast, the tax collector stood away, feeling unclean, condemned. He was so shameful that he could not lift up his head. He just struck his own chest and cried out "God be merciful to me a sinner." Jesus said his prayer was heard, not the Pharisee's. Jesus said the tax collector was justified, not the Pharisee.

Unconditional regard for others begins with a sense of one's own inadequacies. It depends on awareness that we are not perfect; we have not arrived; we do not know all we need to know, or do all that we should do. We are taken with the recognition that we are sinful. This enables the person, with unconditional personal regard, to show patience, to listen intently, and to be vitally interested in the well-being of another.

"Forget not that hast often sinned, And sinful yet thou wilt be;

Deal gently with the erring one, As thy God hath dealt with thee."

(http://womenshistory.about.com/library/etext/poem1/blp_carney, Think Gently of the Erring By Julia Carney, Date Accessed February 21, 2013) .

GROW IN GRACE

But grow in grace, and in the knowledge of our Lord and Saviour Jesus Christ.
II Peter 3:18 (KJV)

A picture portrayed a group of tourists set to enter a city and see the sights. A member of the troupe asked, "Were there any great people born here?" The tour guide quickly responded, "No, only babies."

Human beings are not born full-grown and mature. Life naturally brings growth. From nursing, to clasping, to rolling over, sitting alone, crawling, standing, walking, and running --- physical growth is an amazing thing to watch! Psychological/emotional growth is no less characteristic of human beings. Whether one speaks in Freudian terminology (eros, the life instinct), or Adlerian (the ideal self), or even Rogerian (striving for self-actualization), the implication is the same: people have a natural impulse to grow mentally, psychologically, and emotionally.

It is no less true in the spiritual realm; thus the admonition, "Grow in grace..." Read and reflect on the following scriptures, each of which implies spiritual growth: "For when for the time ye ought to be teachers, ye have need that one teach you again which be the first principles of the oracles of God; ..." (Hebrews 5:12, KJV); "For every one that useth milk is unskillful in the word...he is a babe..." (Hebrews 5:13, KJV); "As newborn babes, desire the sincere milk of the word, that you may grow" (First Peter 2:2, KJV); "Strong meat belongeth to them that are of full age..." (Hebrews 5:14, KJV); "When I was a child, I spake as a child, I understood as a child, I thought as a child: but when I became a man, I put away childish things" (First Corinthians 13:11, KJV).

Spiritual growth is possible! Such growth demands time, patience, energy, devotion, and cooperation with the spiritual life force within us. On a scale of one to five, with one representing spiritual immaturity and five representing a fully mature faith, how would you rank yourself? What specific plans do you have to move up the scale, and grow spiritually?

Let us then approach the throne of grace with confidence, so that we may receive mercy and find grace to help us in our time of need. Hebrews 4:16 (NIV)

How often do you feel as if you are not pure or holy enough to enter God's throne room to seek His help in time of great need? If you are like most followers of Christ, there is often a lingering feeling of shame about asking God for help when failing so miserably in living a sin-free life. Our Father knows of our weakness and tendency to fall prey to sin, but has made a way of escape.

Jesus Christ has paid the price for our sins in full! He was the perfect and unblemished Lamb that was offered up to God to make our redemption possible. No one except Jesus has ever managed to exist on this earth without missing the mark. Our efforts to live up to the standards presented in the Holy Scriptures are well intentioned, but fail we will. This is where the wonderful power of grace and mercy enter into the life of the believer.

It is said that grace is getting what we do not deserve, and mercy is the withholding of what we do deserve. Notice these two words grace and mercy constitute the substance of the message found in Hebrews 4:16. Bring the meaning of these uplifting words to mind the next time you are hesitant to seek God's help in your life. Because of what Jesus has already done, you can enter the throne room with confidence.

NEW EVERY MORNING

It is of the Lord's mercies that we are not consumed, …they are new every morning. Lamentations 3:22-23 (KJV)

Mr. and Mrs. Alva Dover left Oklahoma in the dust bowl days of the 1940s. Farming was ruined; livelihoods were gone. There was little hope to subsist. The Dovers left the arid dust and moved to California. There they gained teaching certificates and soon found jobs teaching school. About forty years later, I sat at their kitchen table for breakfast. Mr. Dover prayed a prayer that I suspected he had prayed many, many times before. I have never forgotten his sincere words: "Kind Heavenly Father, thank you for allowing us to rise from beds of rest to see the light of another day." Alva Dover was acutely aware that the Lord's mercies protect us and provide for us each day.

God's people have made this discovery across the years. God gave manna from heaven each day to the children of Israel as they followed Him through the wilderness. Each morning, families gathered all they needed for that day; on Friday, God sent twice as much, enough for Friday and for the Sabbath Day to follow. In the New Testament, Jesus echoed this truth as He taught His followers to pray "Give us this day our daily bread" (Matthew 6:11, KJV). God's mercies are new and fresh each morning!

As you journey, reflect on all the day-to-day ways that God provides for you. Surely, the unusual and uncommon blessings are more noticeable, but do not overlook the common things, the daily provisions, that are continual evidence of God's faithfulness (Lamentations 3:23b, KJV).

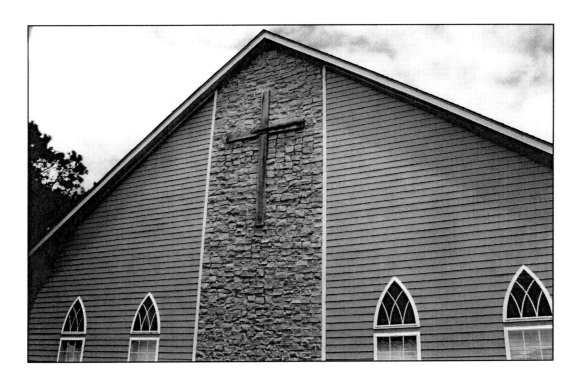

SEEK GOD

If my people, who are called by My Name will humble themselves and pray and seek My Face and turn away from their wicked ways, then I will hear them from heaven and forgive their sin and heal their land. 2 Chronicles 7:14 (NIV)

Are there days when you just shake your head in disbelief about events happening here and throughout the world? Do you ever wonder what happened to acts of kindness and caring about neighbors? Is there any relief for the pain and human suffering we see around us? These are questions that have been asked since humanity populated the earth. Second Chronicles 7:14 gives us some very clear insight into what is wrong and, more important -- how to correct the problem.

King Solomon had just completed building a magnificent temple in which to honor and praise God. But the people under Solomon's rule remained entrenched in evil and disregard for their Heavenly Father. God spoke to Solomon as recorded in Second Chronicles with a message of hope and a prescription for wellness. Even in the most sinful condition of an individual or a society, God's grace and mercy abound.

Repentance is confessing to God that we are regretful of the thoughtless and unloving acts we have committed. It is a humbling experience, and a necessary one to realize forgiveness and healing. Be a part of improving your life, your community, and the world by seeking God's face daily and allowing His presence to guide your steps.

HONOR GOD'S NAME

You shall not misuse the name of the Lord your God, for the Lord will not hold anyone guiltless who misuses His name. Deuteronomy 5: 11 (NIV)

There are several ways God's name is misused and profaned by today's society. We hear some disrespectful phrase daily if we listen closely to the conversations that surround us in restaurants, shopping malls, or in any social gathering. The sin of misusing God's name has even crept, ever so subtly, into the texting world with the exclamation OMG which is often used as a response of surprise in the millions of messages that travel the wireless networks daily.

Do you appreciate someone referring to you, a family member, or friend with a disrespectful term? The answer is no, even if the reference was meant to be humorous and not hurtful. The point here is that all of us, including God Almighty, have a desire to be honored and respected. Our Maker and Creator desires our reverence in communicating in prayer and in all settings. Think before speaking, and demonstrate your love and obedience to God with every word that comes out of your mouth. If you have erred in the past, ask Him for forgiveness and start anew.

IN HIM

For in Him we live, and move, and have our being... Acts 17:28 (KJV)

The apostle was speaking to a large group of very religious people on Mars Hill in Athens. The external trappings of their polytheistic culture were everywhere – temples and idols and altars. Yet Paul seems to be saying, "I see that you practice your religion in a prolific way; just do not miss God! Let me introduce you to Him!"

God is never far away. Frankly, He is ever before us! "In Him we live, and move, and have our being" (verse 28). We are to become Aware of Him, Acquainted with Him, and Absorbed into Him! Being in focus is all-important!

"Earth is crammed with heaven. Every bush is aflame with the fire of God, but only those who see take off their shoes. The rest just pick the berries." --- Elizabeth Browning (http://www.bartleby.com/236/86.html, Date Accessed February 8, 2013)

Are you conscious that you walk on Holy ground? Have you (figuratively) taken off your shoes, as Moses did at the Burning Bush? Are you aware, acquainted and absorbed by/ with God...or just picking berries?

GOD IS GOOD

I will bless the LORD at all times: His praise shall continually be in my mouth.
Psalm 34: 1 (KJV)

"God is good…all the time!" This is a common antiphonal doxology in contemporary worship settings. Someone says "God is good"; others respond "All the time!"

Life may seem uncertain and precarious, even unfair…but God is good…all the time!

People, even relatives, may be forgetful, cruel, mean-spirited and vindictive…but God is good…all the time!

The night may be filled with worry and weeping…but God is good…all the time!

Our hearts may be heavy, crushed with grief, stripped of loved ones…but God is good… all the time!

The psalmist - who experienced all these things - said, "I will bless the LORD at all times: His praise shall continually be in my mouth." Such a focus rises above the ordinary! Such a focus makes life more than mundane! Such a focus -on the Lord- gives us a reason to persevere through difficulty, and to live life to the fullest!

LET OTHERS SEE GOD

No man hath seen God at any time; If we love one another, God dwelleth in us, and His love is perfected in us. 1 John 4:12 (KJV)

The Scriptures declare "God is Spirit" (John 4:24, KJV). Two times, the Bible asserts "no man hath seen God at any time" (John 1:18, KJV; First John 4:12, KJV). However, in the same contexts that say no man has seen God, we are told how we may see Him! John 1:18 (KJV) says "No man hath seen God at any time; the only begotten Son, which is in the bosom of the Father, He hath declared him." This, of course, is speaking of Jesus as the "only begotten Son". Jesus has "declared" God. The root meaning of the word "declared" could be translated "He (Jesus) has spoken God out loud!" The intended impact of that declaration is to say that although God is Spirit, He can be clearly seen in Jesus.

In the second reference (First John 4:12, KJV) that says "No man hath seen God at any time", the writer asserts that God may be seen in the lives of His followers as they love one another. We are never more like the Father than when we love others.

Be encouraged! As you love others and show them respect and unconditional positive regard, they just may see God! And that alone is life-changing!

MATTERS OF THE HEART

I will give them an undivided heart and put a new spirit in them; I will remove from them their heart of stone and give them a heart of flesh. Ezekiel 11:19 (NIV)

In this passage, we find God speaking to the prophet Ezekiel on matters of the heart. Hard- heartedness is a significant problem when it comes to establishing and maintaining a genuine relationship with God and our neighbors. Sometimes this condition goes unnoticed due to lives that are so busy with careers, family, and other self-gratifying activities that our need for a spiritual relationship with our creator is low or non-existent on the list of priorities.

Even with all of the pursuits in search of completeness and satisfaction with life, most of us will continue to experience an inner longing for something more, something deeper, and something profoundly better than what we have. This inner urging is the voice of God speaking and inviting us to come into a complete relationship with Him. He created us to be a part of His family and desires daily contact through our prayers, meditation, and reading of the Word. When we truly love someone, we want to be intimately close and know everything about that person. Allow God to have the place He seeks in your heart and experience the peace and joy that only He can offer. Your consistent fellowship with Him is the best exercise for a warm heart.

LOVING GOD (ONE)

Thou shalt love the Lord thy God with all thy heart, and with all thy soul, and with all thy mind. This is the first and great commandment. Matthew 22: 37-38 (KJV)

The word of God contains many types of messages for you and me. Among the types of messages are the principles of God regarding how to live an effective life during our time here on earth. One of those principles is to love God. The principle of loving God involves several components, a few of which will be highlighted within the next seven meditations and reflections.

To love God. What we believe, what we say, and what we do indicates our level of love for God!

The first component of the principle of loving God involves what you believe regarding the trinity. In Romans 10:9-10 (AMP) we read, "if you acknowledge and confess with your lips that Jesus is Lord and in your heart believe (adhere to, trust in, and rely on the truth) that God raised Him from the dead, you will be saved. For with the heart a person believes (adheres to, trusts in, and relies on Christ) and so is justified (declared righteous, acceptable to God), and with the mouth he confesses (declares openly and speaks out freely his faith) and confirms [his] salvation". Also, in First John 1:9 (AMP) we are told "if we [freely] admit that we have sinned and confess our sins, He is faithful and just (true to His own nature and promises) and will forgive our sins [dismiss our lawlessness] and [continuously] cleanse us from all unrighteousness [everything not in conformity to His will in purpose, thought, and action]".

In John 3:16 (AMP) we learn, "God so greatly loved and dearly prized the world that He [even] gave up His only begotten (unique) Son, so that whoever believes in (trusts in, clings to, relies on) Him shall not perish (come to destruction, be lost) but have eternal (everlasting) life." Scripture goes on to teach us that the Holy Spirit lives within us. Second Timothy 1:14 (NLT) tells us "through the power of the Holy Spirit who lives within us, carefully guard the precious truth that has been entrusted to you."

To love God necessitates that the individual be in relationship with God. At this moment in time, for each person reading the words on this page – the question is, "Have you believed in your heart and confessed with your mouth that Jesus is Lord?"

Selah – pause and think about that.

LOVING GOD (TWO)

Thou shalt love the Lord thy God with all thy heart, and with all thy soul, and with all thy mind. This is the first and great commandment. Matthew 22: 37-38 (KJV)

Another component of the principle of loving God involves believer's baptism. In Matthew 3:13-17 (AMP) we read that Jesus went up to John the Baptist for baptism. Jesus serves as our example regarding baptism.

Baptism is an outward symbol of what occurs spiritually when a person believes in his/her heart and confesses with his/her mouth that Jesus is Lord. Reading Romans 6:3-5 (AMP) provides the best explanation of the symbolic meaning of baptism – "Are you ignorant of the fact that all of us who have been baptized into Christ Jesus were baptized into His death? We were buried, therefore, with Him by baptism into death, so that as Christ was raised from the dead by the glorious [power] of the Father, so we too might [habitually] live and behave in newness of life. For if we have become one with Him by sharing a death like His, we shall also be [one with Him in sharing] His resurrection [by a new life lived for God]."

Loving God involves believer's baptism. The question before you at this moment in time is, "Have you demonstrated your love for God by being baptized?"

LOVING GOD (THREE)

Thou shalt love the Lord thy God with all thy heart, and with all thy soul, and with all thy mind. This is the first and great commandment. Matthew 22: 37-38 (KJV)

Another component of the principle of loving God involves our relationship with other Christians. In First John 4:20 (AMP) we learn, "If anyone says, I love God, and hates (detests, abominates) his brother [in Christ], he is a liar." In John 13:35 (AMP) we read, "by this shall all [men] know that you are My disciples, if you love one another [if you keep on showing love among yourselves]".

Loving God involves loving other Christians. The question before you at this moment in time is "How well do I demonstrate my love for God through the way in which I demonstrate my love for other Christians?"

LOVING GOD (FOUR)

Thou shalt love the Lord thy God with all thy heart, and with all thy soul, and with all thy mind. This is the first and great commandment. Matthew 22: 37-38 (KJV)

Another component of the principle of loving God is that we trust God. Scriptures that clarify how through loving God we trust God are as follows:

1) Psalm 13:5 (KJV)—But I have trusted in Thy mercy; my heart shall rejoice in Thy salvation.

2) Proverbs 3:5 (KJV) – Trust in the Lord with all thine heart; and lean not unto thine own understanding.

3) Psalm 37:3 (KJV) – Trust in the Lord and do good;

4) Psalm 56:4 (KJV) – … in God I have put my trust;

5) Psalm 56:3 (KJV) – What time I am afraid, I will trust in You.

6) Job 13:15 (KJV) – Though He slay me ("even if He kills me" are the words of the Holman Christian Standard Bible, 2009), yet will I trust in Him.

7) John 14:1 (AMP) – Do not let your hearts be troubled (distressed, agitated). You believe in and adhere to and trust in and rely on God;

Loving God involves trusting God. In First Thessalonians 5:18(AMP) we are told to, "Thank [God] in everything [no matter what the circumstances may be, be thankful and give thanks], for this is the will of God for you [who are] in Christ Jesus [the Revealer and Mediator of that will]", and in Romans 8:28 (AMP), "We are assured and know that [God being a partner in their labor] all things work together and are [fitting into a plan] for good to and for those who love God and are called according to [His} design and purpose". Loving God and trusting God "in all circumstances" and "in all things" will be challenging at times. However--- as each of us develops the spiritual and psychological mindset of Job (even if God kills me, yet will I trust Him) --- we will be prepared to meet the challenge.

Loving God involves trusting God. The question before you at this moment in time is, "Are you willing to love and trust God in all circumstances and in all things?"

LOVING GOD (FIVE)

Thou shalt love the Lord thy God with all thy heart, and with all thy soul, and with all thy mind. This is the first and great commandment. Matthew 22: 37-38 (KJV)

Another component of the principle of loving God is that we obey God. Scriptures that clarify how through loving God we obey God are as follows:

1) John 14: 23-24 (AMP) Jesus answered, If a person [really] loves Me, he will keep My word [obey My teaching]; ...Anyone who does not [really] love Me does not observe and obey My teaching.

2) Luke 11:28 (AMP) Blessed (happy and to be envied) rather are those who hear the Word of God and obey and practice it!

3) 1 John 2:4 (AMP) Whoever says, I know Him [I perceive, recognize, understand, and am acquainted with Him] but fails to keep and obey His commandments (teachings) is a liar, and the truth [of the Gospel] is not in him.

4) John 15:10 (AMP) If you keep My commandments [if you continue to obey My instructions], you will abide in My love and live on in it...

5) Acts 10:35 (AMP) But in every nation he who venerates and has a reverential fear of God, treating Him with worshipful obedience and living uprightly, is acceptable to Him and sure of being received and welcomed [by Him].

6) James 2:17 (AMP) So also faith, if it does not have works (deeds and actions of obedience to back it up), by itself is destitute of power (inoperative, dead).

7) 1 John 3:22 (AMP) And we receive from Him whatever we ask, because we [watchfully] obey His orders [observe His suggestions and injunctions, follow His plan for us] and [habitually] practice what is pleasing to Him.

Loving God involves obeying God. The question before you at this moment in time is, "Are you willing to love and obey God in all circumstances and in all things?"

LOVING GOD (SIX)

Thou shalt love the Lord thy God with all thy heart, and with all thy soul, and with all thy mind. This is the first and great commandment. Matthew 22: 37-38 (KJV)

Another component of the principle of loving God is that we serve God. Scriptures that explain how through loving God we serve God are as follows:

1) Mark 10:45 (AMP) For even the Son of Man came not to have service rendered to Him, but to serve , and to give His life as a ransom for (instead of) many.

2) 1 Peter 4:10 (NRSV) Like good stewards of the manifold grace of God, serve one another with whatever gift each of you has received.

3) Romans 7:6 (KJV) But now we are delivered from the law, that being dead wherein we were held; that we should serve in newness of spirit, and not in the oldness of the letter.

4) Hebrews 9:14 (KJV) How much more shall the blood of Christ, who through the eternal Spirit offered Himself without spot to God, purge your conscience from dead works to serve the living God?

5) Romans 12:11 (KJV) Not slothful in business; fervent in spirit; serving the Lord;

6) Galatians 5:13 (KJV) For, brethren, ye have been called unto liberty; only use not liberty for an occasion to the flesh, but by love serve one another.

7) Matthew 6:24 (KJV) No man can serve two masters: for either he will hate the one, and love the other; or else he will hold to one, and despise the other. Ye cannot serve God and mammon.

Loving God involves serving God. The question before you at this moment in time is, "Are you willing to love God and serve God in all circumstances and in all things?"

LOVING GOD (SEVEN)

Thou shalt love the Lord thy God with all thy heart, and with all thy soul, and with all thy mind. This is the first and great commandment. Matthew 22: 37-38 (KJV)

Another component of the principle of loving God is that we give to God. Scriptures that clarify how through loving God we give to God are as follows:

1) Matthew 22:21 (KJV) …Render therefore unto Caesar the things which are Caesar's; and unto God the things that are God's.

2) Proverbs 3:9 (KJV) Honour the Lord with thy substance, and with the first fruits of all thine increase.

3) Malachi 3:10 (AMP) – Bring all the tithes (the whole tenth of your income) into the storehouse, that there may be food in My house, and prove Me now by it, says the Lord of hosts, if I will not open the windows of heaven for you and pour you out a blessing, that there shall not be room enough to receive it.

4) 2 Corinthians 9:6-8 (KJV) …He which soweth sparingly shall reap also sparingly; and he which soweth bountifully shall reap also bountifully. Every man according as he purposeth in his heart, so let him give; not grudgingly, or of necessity; for God loveth the cheerful giver. And God is able to make all grace abound toward you; that ye, always having all sufficiency in all things, may abound to every good work.

5) Luke 6:38 (KJV) Give, and it shall be given unto you; good measure, pressed down, and shaken together, and running over, shall men give into your bosom. For with the same measure that ye mete withal it shall be measured to you again.

6) Matthew 6:3-4 (KJV) But when thou doest alms, let not thy left hand know what thy right hand doeth; that thine alms may be in secret; and thy Father which seeth in secret Himself shall reward thee openly.

7) Hebrews 11:6 (KJV) But without faith it is impossible to please Him; for he that cometh to God must believe that He is, and that He is a rewarder of them that diligently seek Him.

8) 2 Corinthians 8:12 (KJV) For if there be first a willing mind, it is accepted according to that a man hath, and not according to that he hath not.

9) Acts 20:35 (KJV) …It is more blessed to give than to receive.

10) John 3:16 (KJV) For God so loved the world, that He gave His only begotten Son, that whosoever believeth in Him should not perish, but have everlasting life.

Loving God involves giving to God. The question before you at this moment in time is, "Are you willing to love God and give to God in all circumstances and in all things?"

FAITH HOPE LOVE

And now these three remain: faith, hope and love. But the greatest of these is love.
1 Corinthians 13:13 (NIV)

Here, Paul is emphasizing three essential characteristics of a follower of Jesus. In order to walk in His footsteps, we are to become more like Him than our "natural" selves. When we meet with acquaintances and friends, the conversations rarely mirror the talk of people who are filled with faith, hope, and love. It is more likely that we will hear complaints, fear of what the future has in store, and worse--- just plain old gossip about our neighbors.

It is often been said that what comes out of the mouth represents what is in the heart. If we accept this as a truth, it becomes clear that our hearts need mending. Jesus was the perfect representation of faith, hope, and love. He knew that God would always abide within Him. His hope was in the rebirth of every present and future person on earth. His love was so deep and passionate that He chose to go to the cross as a perfect and unblemished sacrifice to pay for the sins of mankind -- forever.

Be aware of the words you speak to yourself and to others. They not only reveal your true character, but also affect your peace, joy, and ability to truly walk in His footsteps. Weigh every word that comes out of your mouth on the scale of faith, hope, and love.

FAITH HOPE EVIDENCE

Now faith is the substance of things hoped for, the evidence of things not seen.
Hebrews 11:1 (NKJV)

In the world in which we exist, we are trained to use our physical senses to guide our footsteps in just about every activity that we engage in. What we can see, touch, smell, taste, and hear become the primary sources by which we define reality. Unshakable credence is placed on concrete, measurable sensory input from the environment that surrounds us. The information is used to guide not only our behavior, but our decisions, as well.

Yet for those who have chosen to follow Christ, the path on which we travel is navigated with an additional source of guidance, faith –"Now faith". God's word contains over 600 promises that apply to those who choose to enter into fellowship with Him. The promises stand as irrefutable evidence of His love and concern for His family in all circumstances. Oftentimes, however, a patient wait precedes answered prayer in order for God's timing to manifest itself. Faith is demonstrated by turning loose of seemingly unsolvable circumstances and demonstrating a willingness to pray and wait for the perfect outcome.

We live in an age of instant gratification and waiting, patiently, is not a well-received or practiced discipline. Solving problems and fulfilling needs is God's specialty. Slow down and train yourself to be patient and faithful in your belief in Him. He can be trusted in all things.

THE SPIRIT OF THE LORD

The Spirit of the Sovereign Lord is on me, because the Lord has anointed me to preach the good news to the poor. He has sent me to bind up the brokenhearted, to proclaim freedom for the captives and release from darkness for the prisoners, to proclaim the year of the Lord's favor and the day of vengeance for our God, to comfort all who mourn and provide for those who grieve in Zion... Isaiah 61: 1 - 3 (NIV)

Do you hear the voice of Jesus speaking through the prophet, Isaiah? That is exactly what is being conveyed in this uplifting verse of scripture from the Old Testament. We have every reason to place our hope and trust in our Lord and Savior for He brings with Him everything that is needed to heal the needy and seemingly hopeless human condition.

The conditions revealed in this passage are experienced by everyone sooner or later as we navigate through our daily lives. Both the saved and the unsaved will experience the dark abyss of fear, failure, grief, and hopelessness. For those who have chosen to abide with Christ, however, He is our constant companion Who will lift us up in all circumstances when we place our faith and trust in Him. His promises are rock-solid. For the unbeliever, help in times of need is often scarce or non-existent.

The deep desire for security and protection is imbedded in every living creature. Turning your heart and life over to Jesus Christ can turn a life of anxiety into one of confidence in the future. If you have not met Jesus, ask Him to come into your life today.

LET THERE BE LIGHT

In the beginning God created the heavens and the earth. Now the earth was formless and empty, darkness was over the surface of the deep, and the spirit of God was hovering over the waters. And God said, "Let there be light," and there was light. Genesis 1: 1-3 (NIV)

The history of our planet, Earth, begins with God speaking light into existence. Before light was created only darkness existed, and the earth was formless and empty. All of God's wonderful creation and the beauty that we observe in nature today would not be marveled at without being preceded by the miracle of light. Light is a powerful and uplifting energy.

Many who read this account of the creation of light have been in a cave designed as a tourist attraction like Carlsbad Caverns in New Mexico or Mammoth Cave in Kentucky. The visitors experience what it is like to be in an environment of total darkness: a place where absolutely no light is present. It is an eerie feeling at best and frightening at worst. The touring groups feel a sense of relief when the lighting system of the cave is finally available once again. The smallest light source like a flashlight will cut through the smothering darkness and raise our spirits.

A life without Christ has many of the same qualities as the cavern experience. It is a dark and unpredictable existence filled with insecurity and a perpetual gnawing angst. When we read God's word and engage Him in conversations through daily prayer, He brings "the light" into our lives just as in the very beginning of creation. It is said in Proverbs that it is better to light one candle than to curse the darkness. Choose to walk in the light of Christ and share the true and eternal source of light with those who know only darkness.

I GIVE YOU POWER

Behold, I give you power…. over all the power of the enemy Luke 10:19(KJV)

But he that glorieth, let him glory in the Lord. II Corinthians 10:17 (KJV)

It was a fine day! A day of celebration! The disciples had come back from a time of ministry during which they had seen miraculous things. They had healed. They had cast out demons. They had "power to tread on serpents and scorpions" (Luke 10:19, KJV). They were giddy in victory! Who would not be? Jesus commended them for their victory over the forces of Satan (Luke 10:18, KJV). He acknowledged the miracles that had been worked at their hand. Then….He put it all in perspective, "…rejoice not that the spirits are subject to you; but rather rejoice because your names are written in heaven"(Luke 10:20, KJV). It was as if He was saying, "Do not be too proud of what you think you have accomplished; be aware that this has been accomplished because of your relationship with God!" It is not your power, but His!

A traveler was thirsty in his journey. He spied in the distance what appeared to be a person standing at the handle of a pump, vigorously pumping water, which gushed out the spout! As the traveler approached closer and closer, he was eager for a drink, and determined that he would stand aside and wait his turn, seeing that the man at the pump continued to pump water. When the traveler arrived at the pump, he made a startling discovery; the "man" was not a real person, but a statue with a hinged arm. The hand at the end of the hinged arm was welded to the pump handle, and as the water from the artesian well surged through the pipe, the force of the water moved the hinged arm up and down! The man was not pumping the water; the water was pumping the man!

Herein is the lesson Jesus seemed to be relating (and illustrated by this parable): when you meet with success, take care not to focus too much on your success; you may think it is all because of you and your abilities. Rather "rejoice that your name is written in heaven"; you have a relationship with God, and any successes you may have are by virtue of His power!

COURAGEOUS AND ENCOURAGING

Be strong and courageous. Do not be afraid because of them for the Lord your God goes before you; He will never leave you nor forsake you. Deuteronomy 31:6 (NIV)

This passage reflects a promise that came from God to Moses. The aging leader was in the process of turning over His leadership role to Joshua when God spoke to him with those reassuring words of presence and protection. After hearing this prophetic declaration, Moses summoned Joshua and all Israel to urge them onward in their journey to the promised land.

Sometimes encouragement is in short supply, in the world in which we live. Our lives are burdened with many have-to activities and a considerable amount of just plain busy work (e.g. spending hours on social media and texting). Imagine what a ministry you could have if you used your time wisely encouraging and uplifting those who are hurting and fearful of what lies ahead. We may not face the many enemies that plotted to thwart Israel's journey to their inheritance, but our paths often seem just as impossible and frightening to navigate.

Perhaps you have a personal need for encouragement in your life and need an uplifting message to move forward. One rich source is found in daily reading of the Bible and a consistent time for daily prayer. Joining together with fellow Christians for prayer and support is another source of strength for facing life's mountains. You will be pleasantly surprised, if not amazed, at the confidence that will flow out of these simple yet profoundly effective strategies.

TRIALS OF LIFE (ONE)

There was a man in the land of Uz, whose name was Job; and that man was perfect and upright, and one that feared God, and eschewed evil. Job 1:1 (KJV)

Though he was a good man, Job suffered. He suffered seven severe tests. Perhaps these seven trials encompass all categories of distress that people face. First was the test of Prosperity. Job was a wealthy man (Job 1:3, KJV). Does prosperity make one generous or greedy? Does prosperity breed the kind of pride that causes people to think they have need of nothing and no one? Or does prosperity bring the realization that every good thing comes from God and that we deserve none of it?

Job faced the test of Adversity. He lost his wealth and possessions (Job 1:14-17, KJV). How do we respond when the stock market falls? When fire destroys the house? When our pay is cut or our job is lost?

Third was the test of Sorrow. His ten children, all of them, were killed as they had a celebration (Job 1:18-21, KJV). Perhaps there is nothing so distressing as the loss of a child. In an ideal world, the young bury the old, but the world is not always ideal.

The fourth test was the challenge of Physical Affliction (Job 2:7, KJV). Job was afflicted with sores and boils --- from head to toe. The Hebrew term is "shehinrac"; it means "to be hot." Job had terrible sores, oozing with infection. He scraped away the pus with sharp pieces of pottery, trying to gain some relief (Job 2:8, KJV).

Time after time, the hammer falls in Job's life. We want to ask, "Why does all this suffering happen? Why do these tests come?" Perhaps the only answer at times is found in Job's declaration: "Man that is born of woman is of few days and full of trouble" (Job 14:1, KJV). Consider the words of Jesus: "In this world you shall suffer tribulation..." (John 16:33, KJV). The question is not whether we will encounter suffering; the greater question is how will we respond to suffering?

Paul was strengthened by the awareness that "the sufferings of this present time are not worthy to be compared with the glory which shall be revealed in us" (Romans 8:18, KJV). Suffering is not only temporary, but the degree of severity in the suffering is more than counterbalanced by the eternal glory awaiting believers!

TRIALS OF LIFE (TWO)

There was a man in the land of Uz, whose name was Job; and that man was perfect and upright, and one that feared God, and eschewed evil. Job 1:1 (KJV)

Job faced the challenges of Prosperity, Adversity, Sorrow, and Physical Affliction. Each took its toll on him. And yet there was deeper, darker, and more challenging to come. Job faced the test of Domestic Tension. Job's wife had the philosophy that life ought to be pleasant all the time, and if it were not, then there is no use living (Job 2:9-10, KJV). This is a widespread philosophy in this day, tragically resulting in high suicide rates. The story of Job is designed in part, to teach us that life is not to be lived on those terms. The reason we are here in this world is not just to have a comfortable, good time! When pressure comes, when life tumbles in and is no longer fun, life is still worth living! It is not uncommon that the greatest challenges to our emotional and spiritual health come from nearby!

Job was confronted by the test of Intellectual Reason in the person of his "three friends" [if you can call them that!] (Job 2:11, KJV). These friends represent a kind of religious orthodoxy, which led them to deduce that Job had sinned and brought these calamities upon himself. Here is an example of their logic: All cows have four legs. Fido has four legs. Therefore, Fido is a cow. Poor, faulty logic! All sin causes suffering; Job's suffering; therefore, Job must have sinned. These friends are the type who probably never had encountered any real trouble, but they have all the answers about your troubles! They talk but do not feel. It could be said that they had absolutely no empathy. They are detached from the reality of suffering.

The greatest test was the Spiritual test. He felt spiritually alone. Job felt God had left him (Job 9:11; 23:3, 8-9, KJV).

Two great foundations help us to persevere when the trials of life come. First, we can endure almost anything if we can find some explanation for it, some reason behind it, some purpose for it. The second is that we can face almost anything if we are not alone. The message of the suffering death of Jesus Christ on the cross is that no person can ever say that he or she is "God-forsaken." On the contrary, Jesus said, "I will never leave you" (Hebrews 13:5, KJV).

COMFORT

"Blessed be the God and Father of our Lord Jesus Christ, the Father of Mercies and the God of all comfort, Who comforts us in all our tribulation, that we may be able to comfort those who are in any trouble, with the comfort by which we ourselves are comforted by God." 2 Corinthians 1: 3-4 (NKJV)

The walk of Jesus during His ministry on earth serves as a testimony to His love of humanity. As our perfect model for the Christian walk, His care and concern about others is everlasting. It speaks to how we should conduct our journey and respond in times of tribulation. Although pain, sorrow, and regrets cannot be avoided -- there is a readily available source of comfort to us through prayer.

In the Gospel of John, Jesus speaks of "the Comforter," or Holy Spirit, that resides within every believer and intercedes for us in both heaven and on earth. We open up communication with the Holy Spirit when we pray and seek His remedy to our problems. In this manner, fear and anxiety are replaced with peace and joy that can come only from Jesus.

Not only should we seek the comfort of Christ in our personal suffering and hardships, but we should be alert and responsive to the needs of others. Share the precious gift of the Comforter with all who are in need. Our walk is about giving as well as receiving. Helping family, friends, and strangers in difficult times is, perhaps, the greatest way to stand as a witness to the power of our Lord and Savior.

LAND OF THE LIVING

[What, What would have become of me] had I not believed that I would see the Lord's goodness in the land of the living! Psalm 27:13 (AMP)

In the book of Job, we read that Job lost all his possessions, lost his family and friends, and lost his health. Had he listened to the advice of his wife, Job would have cursed God and died (Job 2:9, KJV). Fortunately Job trusted God (Job 13:15, KJV) and knew that his redeemer lived (Job19:25, KJV).

There may come times in each of our lives that we experience situations/circumstances that are personally overwhelming, that like Job we think "my soul is weary of my life" (Job 10:1, KJV), --- that make us want to give up and quit life. I have experienced those types of overwhelming situations/circumstances twice in my life. The worst of the two occurred in February 1975. Though overwhelmed psychologically, I was (thankfully) spiritually able to cling to God and hope/believe that I would, once again, see the goodness of the Lord in the land of the living. Now over 35 years later, when I reflect on the years of my life and I think of the scripture "what would have become of me had I not believed that I would see the Lord's goodness in the land of the living" – I can say that because of the hope that the Word of God brought to me in 1975, I have lived to experience the goodness of the Lord in the land of the living.

DO NOT GIVE UP

Let us not become weary in doing good, for at the proper time we will reap a harvest if we do not give up. Galatians 6:9 (NIV)

There are a lot of reasons why we weary or tire of giving of ourselves to others. Sometimes we just are so busy doing good works at the expense of neglecting personal and family needs. We are sensing inner conflict because we have spread ourselves too thin. In other instances, the people we are reaching out to may not express appreciation for what we are trying to do for them – or perhaps resent us as meddling "do-gooders". And yet, another reason we may tire is because of our hidden motivation of expecting God to provide a reward on a timetable that meets our immediate needs and expectations -- thus we are disappointed.

It is important to keep in mind that whenever we are engaged in "doing good" that the drive comes out of our love of Christ and our desire to follow the commandment of "loving our neighbor as ourselves" (Matthew 22:39, NIV). When the motivation is right, we will not tire and become weary because our acts of goodness are supported by the grace of God that is in plentiful supply. We also need to be aware that the "harvest" that comes as a result of doing good comes on God's timetable and in the form of what He knows will bless us! Our Creator strengthens us to accomplish His work and keeps His promises to all who believe in His Son, Jesus Christ.

REJOICE / BE JOYFUL

…yet I will rejoice in the Lord, I will be joyful in God my Savior. Habakuk 3:18 (NIV)

This verse comes from Habakuk, a small book in the Old Testament with a big truth. The verse reminds us of God's reliability in all circumstances. Life is filled with victories and defeats. When you read chapter 3 in its entirety, God's omnipotence and creative power exceed our imagination. In addition to authority and power, we see God's consistency to judge sin and bless the believer.

Life is often described as a roller coaster whose track takes us to the heights of joy and then down to the depths of grief and depression. Though the hills and valleys of our existence are not likely to be completely removed, we can make them less radical by trusting God's promise of protection in all circumstances. Yes, it is difficult to get our mind off of the problems we face when they threaten our families, health, or livelihood. Our tendency is to obsessively meditate on the problems and often "grow" them into immense proportions. The good news is that you can do something to overcome the worries of the world.

We are instructed in the Word that we can count on the reliability of God's promises for us. Discovering the certainty of deliverance and protection from our detractors is found throughout the scriptures. If you are experiencing anguish as the result of your circumstances, start with spending some time in the Psalms. These uplifting words of God will help you develop your confidence and strength to withstand and overcome all that comes against you.

I AM WHAT I AM

But by the grace of God I am what I am, and His grace to me was not without effect. No, I worked harder that all of them – yet not I, but the grace of God that was with me.
1 Corinthians 15:10 (NIV)

The Apostle Paul knew full well that his life, his accomplishments, and his ministry success all came from God's grace. He understood God's greatness and that nothing exists or happens that is not in the ultimate control and plan of the Creator. This is an extremely difficult concept for us to grasp – until something goes wrong in our personal world.

We tend to be a proud, independent, and prideful people who not only boast about our personal wealth and accomplishment; but we also like to secretly think we are doing God a favor by helping someone in need or, perhaps, dropping a twenty in the offering on Sunday. The reality is that God does not need us, but we desperately need Him; for it is our Father in Heaven that brings all good things into existence.

Whatever goodness you have or will experience in life is God's gift at Christ's expense. Approach His throne with humility and offer daily thanks for the wonderful gifts that have been given to you. Be gracious and share your bounty whenever possible -- giving all credit, glory, and honor to God Almighty.

…we were pressed out of measure, above strength, insomuch that we despaired even of life. II Corinthians 1:8 (KJV)

Was it physical distress? The writer had been stoned, dragged out of the city, and left for dead. Was it psychological and emotional? Paul had been chased and hounded all across Asia, ridiculed and accused as he endeavored to carry the message of the gospel. Perhaps it was both physical and mental distress that brought him low. Whatever the burden, whatever the affliction he spoke of and was facing, it had brought him to the precipice of despair. He felt that his life could not go on. He thought his life would not go on. He had gone his last mile.

On your journey through life, you will meet many people who have felt just as Paul. You will meet many at the very time they despair of life, at the moment when they feel they have reached the end of their rope. It is not an easy place to be. Perhaps even you will "hit the bottom" at some point.

Indeed, life can be characterized by the phrase "high mountains, low valleys." Great victories are sometimes followed by failure. Service to others is often unappreciated and may even be resented and resisted. Trust placed in another person is sometimes betrayed. We even disappoint ourselves. Simon Peter, after so adamantly insisting that he would never deny Christ, and asserting that he was willing to die with Him, if necessary, within twenty-four hours denied that he even knew Christ. He denied three times, and he "wept bitterly", perhaps "despairing of life."

What will you do when you walk through this valley of despair? Paul said, "We had this sentence of death in ourselves, that we should not trust in ourselves, but in God which raiseth the dead" (II Corinthians 1:9, KJV). God, who raises the dead, can also raise us up out of the valley of despair! Jesus had told Simon Peter, "Simon, behold, Satan hath desired to have you, that he may sift you as wheat : But I have prayed for thee, that thy faith fail not: and when thou art converted, strengthen thy brethren" (Luke 22:31, KJV). God is for you! He Who raises the dead is with you! As you trust Him, He will be with you through this valley of despair and beyond!

GET UP AND GO

And God is able to make all grace abound to you, so that in all things at all times, having all that you need, you will abound in every good work. 2 Corinthians 9:8 (NIV)

The Christian's life journey involves more than simply accepting the good things God provides. We are equipped not only with material possessions but also with special gifts to carry out the mission of helping others, by meeting their needs and sharing the good news of God's redemptive power. This is how we become Christ's disciples – by moving out of the comfort zone and onto the battlefield of where we are in life.

Most of us minimize our skills, talents and abilities and have difficulty clearly identifying the areas in which we can become His servants. Serving God does not require any more expertise and resources than are already in your possession. We feel to be of value, we need to do something big, something important or complicated. Thoughts of inadequacy for the job will paralyze our efforts with inertia – the tendency of a body at rest is to remain in that state.

More than ever our world today needs you and every other sojourner to reach out and influence others for Christ by demonstrating our love through giving and service. Keep in mind that God will not ask nor require you to do anything beyond your capacity. He gives you everything needed by His grace. The only requirement is that you listen for His voice to guide you -- and get up and go!

KEEPING ON   KEEPING ON

I have glorified Thee on the earth; I have finished the work which Thou gavest me to do. John 17:4(KJV)

Everyone is motivated about something; some are motivated for ten minutes; some for two weeks; some for perhaps a year. Those who accomplish the most – those who make the greatest impact-- are those who maintain motivation for ten, twenty, thirty years or more!

At this point in the life of Jesus, it was a done deal. Jesus had "set His face" to go to Jerusalem to be crucified. He had wrestled in the Garden of Gethsemane with abandonment of this consuming purpose. Yet He had said, "Thy will be done"….and He meant it.

It is this kind of all-out commitment, this type of compelling purpose, which perseveres and finishes. Those who feel called to be helpers, like counselors, often face challenges to perseverance. Lack of support, modest incomes, client resistance, long hours, dangerous encounters, and the list can go on and on--- create an urge within to go in another direction.

The distinct impression that God has called you, that He has given you this work, can enable you to press on! Re-discover that sense of purpose and calling, and glorify the One Who gave it to you, by keeping on keeping on!

JUSTIFICATION   SANCTIFICATION   GLORIFICATION

Being confident of this thing, that He which hath begun a good work in you will perform it until the day of Jesus Christ. Philippians 1:6 (KJV)

"Justification…Sanctification…Glorification." These three big, "churchy" words are loaded with meaning and significance. "Justification" is the process by which God absolves believers from all sin. "Christ died for our sins" (First Corinthians 15:3, KJV). In a much deeper way than the human mind can comprehend, the death of Jesus on the cross was a substitution for the sins of all humans of all time, and, therefore, He paid the penalty of death for our sins (Romans 3:24-26, KJV). God began His good work in you when you became a believer in Jesus Christ!

God will also "carry it on to completion" (Philippians 1:6, KJV). This ongoing work of God within believers is called "sanctification." The root word of "sanctification" is the same word as "holy". It means to separate or set apart. Believers are once-and-for-all set apart unto God (Hebrews 10:10, KJV). It is also an ongoing process (John 17:16, KJV) by which believers grow in grace and in their separation unto God. So God's work in and for us is an Event (justification) followed by a Process (sanctification).

"Glorification" is the consummation of God's work in us. Believers are changed "from glory to glory" (II Corinthians 3:18, KJV) until we are made like Christ (Colossians 1:27; 3:4, KJV; I John 3:2, KJV). Romans 8:30(KJV) contains a powerful truth: "Those He justified, them He also glorified." These words are written in the perfect tense in the Greek language, implying an action completed in the past, with lasting and continuing results. So as far as God is concerned, the ultimate salvation of believers, transformation into the likeness of Christ to live eternally, is as good as done! It is done! It has already been completed! It is finished! What God began, He will carry through!

WAITING ON GOD

Yet the Lord longs to be gracious to you; He rises to show you compassion. For the Lord is a God of justice. Blessed are all who wait for Him! Isaiah 30: 18 (NIV)

Patience, patience, patience! Do you remember your parents repeating these words when you were a child and wanted an immediate response to your demand? Waiting for gratification or fulfillment of a request is not well-received by children, or for that matter, by most adults. We want what we want, when we want it!

When all is going smoothly and problem-free in our lives, there is generally a dearth of communication occurring between us and our heavenly Father. As soon as troubled times and crisis arrive at our front door, the communication line between earth and heaven gets very busy with pleas for deliverance from our woes. How easy it is to forget that the grace of God is always operative. It never leaves us as members of His family.

The prophet Isaiah reminds us that our God is full of grace, compassion, and will see that justice is delivered. He also tells us very clearly that waiting patiently is also to be expected. In other words, God cannot be badgered, bribed, begged, or rushed into solving our problems the moment our petitions are made. The time between problem and a solution is often used to remind us of God's sovereignty and our inability to control outcomes on demand. Remind yourself frequently: blessed are all who wait for Him!

YOU ARE A LETTER

You show that you are a letter from Christ, the result of our ministry, written not with ink but with the Spirit of the living God, not on tablets of stone but on tablets of human hearts. 2 Corinthians 3:3 (NIV)

What a beautiful way of describing how we should present ourselves to the world as brothers and sisters in Christ. Paul is emphasizing that our head knowledge of the tenets of the Christian faith is not enough. We must also express and practice those beliefs in our everyday behavior. It is the greatest challenge we face in our daily walk with Jesus.

Paul's challenge to the Corinthians is just as valid today in the world in which we live. If we can learn not just to "talk the talk," but instead "walk the talk" --- we can become a powerful witness for Christ. Think about it for a moment, are you not drawn to people who are strong in practicing their faith through action and not through empty words? If you have allowed Jesus to come into your heart, you have accepted the work of becoming a minister of the Gospel. As a minister of the Gospel, you are a letter from Christ to others.

God has equipped you sufficiently to bring the good news to everyone you meet. We just need to remember that our behavior toward others is a true indication of what is in our hearts. Examine your responses toward those you meet on a daily basis. Are you exhibiting a loving and caring demeanor? Are you able to demonstrate empathy for the needs of others? These are the keys to experiencing an effective ministry for Christ. He said, "My grace is sufficient for you, for my power is made perfect in your weakness" (Second Corinthians 12:9, NIV).

FORGIVENESS (ONE)

Pray, therefore, like this: Our Father, Who is in heaven, hallowed (kept holy) be Your name. Your kingdom come, Your will be done on earth as it is in heaven. Give us this day our daily bread. And forgive us our debts, as we also have forgiven (left, remitted, and let go of the debts, and have given up resentment against) our debtors. And lead (bring) us not into temptation, but deliver us from the evil one. For Yours is the kingdom and the power and the glory forever. Amen. Matthew 6: 9-13 (AMP)

The word of God contains many types of messages for you and me. Among the types of messages are the principles of God regarding how to live an effective life during our time here on earth. One of those principles is forgiveness. The principle of forgiveness involves several components, a few of which will be highlighted within the next seven meditations and reflections.

Forgive us our debts, as we also have forgiven our debtors. The New Living Translation (2007) states it using more modern language, "Forgive us our sins as we have forgiven those who sin against us." We are forgiven based upon how well we forgive others.

So the first component of the principle of forgiveness involves each of us examining ourselves in light of how well we forgive others. When we examine ourselves in light of how well we forgive others, we should always remember the level of forgiveness we are asking God for in light of our past and present levels of sin (both commission and omission) – as well as our sin debt that awaits us in our future.

Forgive us our sins, as we have forgiven those who sin against us. The question before you at this moment is, "How well do you forgive others?"

FORGIVENESS (TWO)

…Forgive us our sins, as we have forgiven those who sin against us…
Matthew 6:12 (NLT)

Another component of the principle of forgiveness involves confessing our sins to God. "If we [freely] admit that we have sinned and confess our sins, He is faithful and just [true to His own nature and promises] and will forgive our sins [dismiss our lawlessness] and [continuously] cleanse us from all unrighteousness [everything not in conformity to His will in purpose, thought and action] (First John 1:9, AMP). IF we confess our sins, THEN God will forgive us and cleanse us from all unrighteousness.

We confess our sins to God because it is against God, and God only, that we have sinned (Psalm 51:4, AMP). Jesus is the atoning sacrifice for our sins and the sins of the world (First John 2:2, AMP). As the words of the hymn, *There is Power in the Blood*, so magnificently declare, "Would you be free from the burden of sin…come for a cleansing to Calvary's tide" (Baptist Hymnal, 1956, edited by Walter Hines Sims, by Lewis E. Jones).

Forgive us our sins, as we have forgiven those who sin against us. The question before you at this moment is "Are you willing to confess your sins to God and ask for forgiveness?"

FORGIVENESS (THREE)

…Forgive us our sins, as we have forgiven those who sin against us…
Matthew 6:12 (NLT)

Another component of the principle of forgiveness involves not only confessing our sins to God, but a desire and willingness to forsake the sin (Proverbs 28:13, AMP). The process of forsaking the sin brings in the doctrine of sanctification (please review the meditation/reflection "Justification, Sanctification, Glorification") – but for now the focus is simply on the individual's desire. Does the individual desire to forsake the sin?

The person who desires to forsake the sin, but experiences major challenges in finding success, can find comfort in the words of Paul when he shares "I fail to practice the good deeds I desire to do, but the evil deeds that I do not desire to do are what I am [ever] doing" (Romans 7:19, AMP). As we continue to explore the principle of forgiveness in light of the doctrine of sanctification and the words of Paul in Romans 7, the light needed for this aspect of the journey will emerge. For now, let us cling to God's mercy and grace for our failures (Hebrews 4:16, KJV).

Forgive us our sins as we have forgiven those who sin against us. The question before you at this moment is, "Do you desire to forsake the sin?"

FORGIVENESS (FOUR)

...Forgive us our sins, as we have forgiven those who sin against us...
Matthew 6:12 (NLT)

Another component of the principle of forgiveness involves understanding what God does with our sin once we have confessed our sin. Some key verses regarding the forgiveness that each of us receives from God and that need to become part of our daily thought process are as follows:

A) Psalm 86:5 (AMP) – For You, O Lord, are good, and ready to forgive [our trespasses, sending them away, letting them go completely and forever]; and you are abundant in mercy and loving kindness to all those who call upon you.

B) Psalm 103:12 (AMP) -- As far as the east is from the west, so far has He removed our transgressions from us.

C) Micah 7:19 (AMP) -- ... He will subdue and tread underfoot our iniquities. You will cast all our sins into the depth of the sea.

D) Jeremiah 31:34 (AMP) -- ... For I will forgive their iniquity, and I will [seriously] remember their sin no more.

E) Hebrews 10:17 (AMP) -- ... their sins and their lawbreaking I will remember no more.

Forgive us our sins, as we have forgiven those who sin against us. The question before you at this moment is, "Do you desire to forgive others in the same way God forgives you?"

FORGIVENESS (FIVE)

…Forgive us our sins, as we have forgiven those who sin against us…
Matthew 6:12 (NLT)

Another component of the principle of forgiveness involves distinguishing between conviction and condemnation. Cindy Wright of the Marriage Missions writes, "Conviction is from the Holy Spirit, prompting us to confess and be restored to fellowship with God…its purpose is to draw us closer to God. Condemnation is from Satan, trying to convince us that we are no good, and that God will never forgive us. Its purpose is to keep us away from God by making us feel guilty" (www.marriagemissions.com, Discerning the difference between the conviction of the Holy Spirit and condemnation of the enemy, Date Accessed, November 14,2012). Some key verses regarding conviction/condemnation that the word of God provides for us and that need to become part of our daily thought process are as follows:

A) Romans 2:4 (NIV) – Or do you show contempt for the riches of His kindness, tolerance, and patience, not realizing that God's kindness leads you toward repentance.

B) 1 John 1:9 (ESV) – If we confess our sins, He is faithful and just to forgive us our sins and to cleanse us from all unrighteousness.

C) John 12:47 (ISV) -- …I did not come to condemn the world but to save it.

D) Romans 8:1 (NLT) -- So now there is no condemnation for those who belong to Christ Jesus.

E) Philippians 3:13 (NLT) – No, dear brothers and sisters, I am still not all I should be, but I am focusing all my energies on this one thing: forgetting the past and looking forward to what lies ahead.

Forgive us our sins, as we have forgiven those who sin against us. The question before you at this moment is, "Can you distinguish conviction from condemnation, can you respond appropriately to conviction, and can you respond appropriately to condemnation?"

FORGIVENESS (SIX)

...Forgive us our sins, as we have forgiven those who sin against us...
Matthew 6:12 (NLT)

Another component of the principle of forgiveness involves developing the spiritual/psychological mindset of who we are as we embrace the love, mercy, grace, and forgiveness of God. In Second Corinthians 3:18 (The Message) we learn, "as God enters our lives, we become like Him." To develop this spiritual/psychological mindset, one must learn to incorporate the practice of meditation into one's daily routine. Joyce Meyer defines meditate as "to roll over and over in your mind, to mutter, converse aloud with oneself, or declare something" (2012, Change Your Words, Change Your Mind, page 62). To incorporate the practice of meditation into our daily routine will require some creative modifications to the customary way of approaching daily life, but we already know that we are to pray without ceasing (First Thessalonians 5:17,KJV).

The spiritual/psychological mindset that each of us needs to focus on developing, especially when confronted with challenges regarding our individual forgiveness, involves meditating on the fact that each of us has been made righteous. In Second Corinthians 5:21 (NIV) we learn, "God made Him who had no sin to be sin for us, so that in Him we might become the righteousness of God." You and I have been made the righteousness of God through Christ Jesus. Imagine how the inclusion of that one meditation/reflection --- if it became a part of our daily routine --- could impact our life over the course of our journey.

Forgive us our sins, as we have forgiven those who sin against us. The question before you at this moment is, "Are you willing to devote the time and energy required to develop the self-discipline of meditating/reflecting on the Word of God as a way of talking with as well as listening to God regarding anything and everything that He may wish to communicate – including the reality that you have been made the righteousness of God through Christ Jesus for a purpose?"

FORGIVENESS (SEVEN)

…Forgive us our sins, as we have forgiven those who sin against us…
Matthew 6:12 (NLT)

Another component of the principle of forgiveness involves wholistically understanding forgiveness, and allowing that understanding to impact our thoughts, feelings, and behaviors for the building of the Kingdom of God here on earth. A brief review of the components of the principle of forgiveness is as follows:

A) How well do you forgive others?

B) Are you willing to confess your sins to God and ask for forgiveness?

C) Do you desire to forsake the sin?

D) Do you desire to forgive others in the same way God forgives you?

E) Can you distinguish conviction from condemnation, can you respond appropriately to conviction, and can you respond appropriately to condemnation?

F) Are you willing to devote the time and energy required to develop the self-discipline of meditating/reflecting on the word of God as a way of talking with as well as listening to God regarding anything and everything that He may wish to communicate – including the reality that you have been made the righteousness of God through Christ Jesus for a purpose?

In Ecclesiastes 12:13 (KJV) we read, "Let us hear the conclusion of the whole matter: Fear God, and keep His commandments; for this is the whole duty of man." In Matthew 22:36-40 (KJV) we are instructed to love God and to love our neighbor. As part of our purpose while here on earth, each individual needs to participate in the Great Commission as found in the Gospel of Matthew, "Go then and make disciples of all the nations"… (Matthew 28:19-20, AMP). Go then and make disciples may require tremendous sacrifice on your part – maybe even the giving of your life, as in the case of Jim Elliot (http://en.wikipedia.org/wiki/jim_elliot; Philip James Elliot, Missionary Killed in 1956 While on a Mission Trip in Ecuador). However, "go then and make disciples" may require you to simply show/share the love of God by "going about doing good" and/or through random acts of kindness (paying it forward) in your home, community, state, nation, and/or other nations into which God provides the opportunities for you to go.

Forgive us our sins, as we have forgiven those who sin against us. The question before you at this moment is, "Are you willing to become actively involved in sharing the love, grace, mercy, and forgiveness of God that has been made available to each of us through the atoning/redemptive work of Jesus Christ at Calvary through a personal relationship with God and active participation in helping to build the Kingdom of God here on earth?"

TWO BETTER THAN ONE

Two are better than one! Ecclesiastes 4:9-12 (KJV)

Why are "two better than one"? (Ecclesiastes 4:9, KJV). Listen to these reasons from Ecclesiastes!

If one falls down, the other can lift him up (Ecclesiastes 4:10, KJV).

If one is alone when he falls, there is no one to pick him up (Ecclesiastes 4:10,KJV).

Certainly, we each have responsibilities that are for us and no one else. Yet, we cannot do what we do without the support of others. When Emmitt Smith (www.nytimes.com/1994/01/26/sports/super-bowl-xxviii-cowboy-offensive-line-sheds-anonymity-but-not_pounds.html; Date Accessed February 14,2013), of the Dallas Cowboys, was the leading rusher in the National Football League, the first thing he did was buy an expensive gift for all of the offensive linemen who had blocked and cleared the way for him. He knew he did not gain success alone!

If one person would be overtaken and overpowered by another, two would be able to withstand such an attack, and if you have a rope with three strands, it is not easily broken (Ecclesiastes 4:12, KJV)! We are called to help others, to support others, to strengthen others. Jackie Robinson was the first black player to play baseball in the major leagues. Of course, he had a rough time because he was black. He played in Brooklyn for the Dodgers. He played third base. One day he made an error. The fans were very rude to him; they booed, jeered, and cursed. The shortstop was Herman Reese (PeeWee), a very popular player. As the people booed and jeered, Reese called time out and walked over and put his arm around the shoulder of Jackie Robinson. The booing stopped. Jackie Robinson (www.nytimes.com/specials/baseball/bbo-reese-robinson.html, Date Accessed February 14, 2013) said he could never have kept playing baseball if it were not for what PeeWee Reese did that day! Two are better than one!

RIGHT PRIORITY

I am the Lord your God, who brought you out of Egypt, out of the land of slavery. You shall have no other gods before Me. Deuteronomy 5: 6-7 (NIV)

Getting things in the right order and priority is important if we want to live without undue chaos and wrong decision-making. Order and priority are also important to God. A study of the Ten Commandments reveals that the first four are aimed at instructing us on how we are to honor the Father and respect Him. Hence, we have an established priority created by God for our instruction.

The first Commandment tells us that our Heavenly Father wants our undivided devotion; No other gods and no carved images are to take His place. When we view God from this perspective, He becomes our trusted source for fulfilling all needs. When we believe otherwise, we are said to be "double-minded" or believing in Him only when we cannot have our needs met through our own efforts and resources. God hates idolatry and demands our total trust and reliance -- in return God shows exceeding love to those who keep His Commandments.

You may not think that such blatant idolatry exists in modern times, but think again. The love of money, possessions, and power is a root form of idolatry that exists today-- and is no different from what Adam and Eve's transgression represented in the Garden of Eden, or the sins of the generations that followed. Think about where God stands in your priority list; and make sure He is number one.

SEEN AND NOT SEEN

While we look not at the things which are seen, but at the things which are not seen...
II Corinthians 4:18 (KJV)

It was Robert Kennedy (www.brainyquote.com/quotes/r/robertkenn121273; Date Accessed February 8, 2013) who said (paraphrase) "Some people look at things as they are and ask 'Why?' Others look at things that could be and ask 'Why not?"! It is a good day for a person (and for counselors!) when that person no longer concentrates on existing circumstances and begins to envision possibilities! In essence, this is what goal-setting is all about --- seeing the invisible!

Focus only on the visible leads to stagnation; seeing the invisible leads to regeneration. Focus only on the visible leads to depression and despair; focus on the invisible leads to encouragement and renewal! You must see the possibilities, see what does not yet exist, design it in your mind, and take steps to make it visible!

You cannot live your life only by what you can see! Jim Valvano, renowned basketball coach for North Carolina State, NCAA championship coach, Hall of Fame coach, succumbed to cancer at an early age. In one of the most inspirational addresses in modern times, he admitted that anyone could see that cancer was wrecking his body. Yet there was so much more than the eye could see; Valvano (www.brainyquote.com/quotes/authors/j/ jim_valvano.html, Date Accessed February 8, 2013) said, "It cannot touch my heart, my mind, my soul!"

You cannot go just by what you see! What do you envision for your own life....for your family and loved ones....for your clients? Look at those unseen things and ask, "Why not?"!

BELIEVE GOD

…Abraham believed God, and it was imputed unto him for righteousness;
James 2:23(KJV)

Abraham's greatest moments were moments when he exercised great faith. He heard the call of God to leave his home and follow God, and he believed God and obeyed Him, not even knowing where it would lead him (Hebrews 11:8, KJV).

To every person is given a measure of faith (Romans 12:3, KJV), the ability to believe in something or someone. We exercise or express this faith in everyday, mundane ways. For example, we go to see a medical doctor, who writes a prescription for us that we cannot read; we hand it over to a pharmacist whom we may not know; we receive a bottle of pills or other medicine that we cannot pronounce, and we take that medicine as prescribed…believing it will do us great good! That is a lot of faith!

We get in our automobile, place the key in the ignition, and turn the key, believing that the engine will start, and we will be on our way. That is everyday faith; it counts for a lot as we navigate throughout each day.

What counts eternally is to place our faith in God! Trusting God and doing what He says are indications that we are in a right relationship with God. As with Abraham, so with us – believing God is counted as righteousness! Be at peace.

LOOK TO THE FUTURE

Forget the former things; do not dwell on the past. Isaiah 43:18 (NIV)

Here, God is speaking to the Israelites to take their attention away from what He has already done and, instead, to focus on the future where they will see even greater things occur through His power and majesty. Do you wonder why He even had to make this declaration given His constant provision, protection, and blessings for the chosen people?

If you think about it a few moments, you will see that we are much like the people that God led out of the wilderness. It is easy to look back and see the good things God has done for us, but it is not so easy to believe that He is with us today and tomorrow as we struggle with our failures and fears. Past actions of grace are most appreciated, yet we must have faith that He will continue to do great and wonderful works. The Bible describes faith as, "…the substance of things hoped for; the evidence of things unseen" (Hebrews 11:1, KJV).

Constant reminiscing on the past is like driving using the rear view mirror. We need to look at it periodically, but if we keep our focus there too long we risk catastrophe. God is always true to His word. Our task is to remain faithful for His presence and protection today and in the future.

PRAY PRESENT FUTURE

Neither pray I for these alone, but for them also which shall believe… John 17:20 (KJV)

In the context of this scripture (John 17:12-26, KJV), Jesus is praying for His disciples. He affirms that they are safe ("…none of them is lost"- 17:12). He prays that they might have fullness of joy (13). He asks that His followers might be kept from evil (15). Jesus prays that the truth might "sanctify" them, set them apart (17). He acknowledges that they have a divine purpose in the world, much as He did (18).

Then, suddenly, Jesus looks into the future! He becomes farsighted, seeing into the years and ages to come: "I pray for all those who will believe." He envisions that His present company of disciples will join with those who will believe in the future in a divine unity ("that they all may be one…"- 17:21-22). He exuberantly expresses His desire to be with them, all of them from the present into the future, and that they all will know His glory and reflect His love!

It is so very easy to become lost in the mundane and minutia of the everyday. We make lists of things to accomplish today; it is exceptional to reflect on how the momentary fits into the momentous! Every hour and every day are blips on a much bigger timeline! Every encounter today prepares for tomorrow's encounters! Ultimately, as we see ourselves today in the flow of God's grand and eternal purpose, that flow into the vast ocean of cosmic unity, sublime joy, and glorious love! Spend time imagining how your life, today, fits into the greater eternal purposes of God!

YEAR OF OUR LORD

For to you is born this day in the town of David a Savior, Who is Christ (the Messiah) the Lord! Luke 2:11 (Amp)

As I am in the process of writing this meditation/reflection, all around we are preparing to celebrate Christmas in just a few days. The birth of Jesus used to be what provided the basis of our date system. BC represented Before Christ and AD represented Anno Domini or Year of our Lord (http://agards-bible-timeline.com/q4_ad_bc_ce.html, date accessed December 15, 2012). However, in today's world there is a lot of revisionism occurring that is seeking to erase the Christian influence from cultural history.

In today's world, BC has been replaced with the letters BCE (before common era), and AD has been replaced with the letters CE (common era). No mention of Christ, and no mention of our Lord regarding how the dating system was established historically. The year is still 2012, but supposedly not the year of our Lord – but the year of the common era. With revisionism trying to erase the year of our Lord or any mention of Jesus Christ --- and substituting the words common era, perhaps Christians should consider alternatives regarding this concept so as NOT to lose the facts of history.

The year of our Lord versus the year of the common era. Since the letters BCE and CE may be here to stay, I would like to suggest an alternative mental meaning to the letters BCE and CE. BCE stands for Before Christ Entered and CE stands for Christ Entered.

The letters BC and AD may have been changed to BCE and CE, but the date system that utilizes the birth of Jesus Christ as the event that marks the division of how historical time is represented can remain the same. BCE – Before Christ Entered, and CE – Christ Entered. An alternative is to use BCE and CE, but with both definitions of the letters being provided. Individuals who would be offended by the words Jesus Christ can have their definition, and the Christians who desire not to have the historical basis of the date system lost can have their definition. Individuals can choose for him/her self the meaning of the letters BCE and CE --- thus providing American Freedom of Choice and American Political Correctness, without offending either group of people, and without promoting ignorance regarding the historical basis of the date system for the sake of American Political Correctness.

SELAH – pause and think about that.

GOD'S PURPOSE

As he neared Damascus on his journey, suddenly a light from heaven flashed around him. He fell to the ground and heard a voice say to him, "Saul, Saul, why do you persecute Me?" Who are you, Lord", Saul asked. "I am Jesus whom you are persecuting," He replied. "Now get up and go into the city, and you will be told what you must do." Acts 9: 3-6 (NIV)

This is the story of Paul's conversion on his way to Damascus. He was known as Saul at the time and was a zealous follower of Jewish law and excelled as a rabbinical student. His personal mission was to hunt down anyone who belonged to "The Way" and take them as prisoners. Instead, he was knocked to the ground and blinded by the power of God, and was led by hand by his traveling companions to complete his journey to Damascus. Our Father had other plans for Saul.

Sometimes God has to take radical measures to get our attention so that we can do the work that He desires us to accomplish. Like Saul, we often tend to pursue our own passions with the same zeal even when God is gently whispering His need for us to change direction for the accomplishment of His will. As long as we remain bent on fulfilling our own desires and as long as we feel we are in charge of our destiny, we are of little use in completing God's purpose. While our personal mission in the service of our Lord may not be as profound as Paul's, it is an important one, nonetheless. Pray daily for guidance to lead your footsteps down the path God has chosen for you.

GOD'S FREEDOM

Everything is permissible – but not everything is beneficial. Everything is permissible - but not everything is constructive. Nobody should seek His own good, but the good of others. 1 Corinthians 10:23,24 (NIV)

To the non-believer, the Holy Bible is perceived as a book of rules that take the spontaneity and joy out of life. There appears to be many" do nots" and not enough "do's". In actuality, the Word internalized is a gift of freedom that comes from the grace of God. As the Apostle Paul instructs us in Corinthians, he makes it clear that our freedom must be used with prudence and sensitivity and in consideration of the beliefs and feelings of others.

After all, if we are to take the charge of the Great Commission seriously, we will be in the company of people from different ethnic, religious, and social practices. We open the door to good communication by avoiding the use of our freedoms at the expense of inhibiting the development of a relationship. The opportunity to share with others the blessings of our experiences, with God, are far more fruitful when a friendly, accepting tone is set with those we meet in our daily lives. Remembering Paul's instruction will go a long way in enhancing your friendships and your witness to those who do not know Christ.

THE SPIRITUAL STRUGGLE

Finally, be strong in the Lord and in His mighty power. Put on the full armor of God so that you can take a stand against the devil's schemes. For our struggle is not against flesh and blood, but against the rulers, against the authorities, against the powers of this dark world and against the spiritual forces of evil in the heavenly realms. Ephesians 6: 10-12 (NIV)

We are challenged, by the Apostle Paul, to be on-guard against evil forces working in both the heavens and here on earth and to put on the full armor of God in preparation against the inevitable attacks. Satan's work in the convicted Christian's life will often take on the intensity of a war. His stratagems will be aimed at exploiting our every weakness and fear so as to pull us away from our dependency upon God and diminish our confidence in Him as our defender.

Satan does not concentrate nor waste his efforts on the marginal Christian, i.e. the "Sunday Morning Christian." Satan's focus is on the prayer warriors; the generous; the faithful; those who are fully committed to living their lives in obedience to Jesus Christ. Paul wants us to understand that our walk of faith will be subject to the violent attacks from Satanic forces and to be prepared to fight with the heart knowledge that God will see that we emerge victorious. For comfort and confidence in times of attack, turn to the Psalms that have many rich examples of God's power to deliver you from evil.

ETERNAL OPTIC

In the beginning was the Word… John 1:1 (KJV)

The word "Word" in John 1:1 translates the Greek "logos." The Greeks used the term "logos" to mean "reason" or "reasoning". It could mean the "principle of revelation." The logos is the underlying, supportive principle of the universe. The logos "grasps and shapes reality" (Paul Tillich, 1967, Systematic Theology, page 75). John uses this idea to make a powerful deductive declaration. John says the Word (logos) is eternal: "In the beginning was (always) the Word…" (John 1:1, KJV). The Word was always alongside God: "the Word was with God…" The Word has a divine origin: "the Word as (always) God." Then, as eternity further appeared in time, the "Word became flesh and tabernacled among us" (John 1:14, KJV). The very basis and foundation of the universe, the foundation and reason of and for our being, is declared to be God. When one finds this to be true experientially and personally, there is a fundamental change in worldview. People are viewed differently. Time is viewed differently. Events in time – temporal events-- are viewed differently. An eternal optic is gained! Significance is added to existence! Yes, there is more to people than meets the eye! There is a far greater significance to the events and interchanges of life than simply a coincidental meeting or exchange!

I WILL ANSWER

Call unto me, and I will answer you, and will show you great and mighty things which you do not know. (Jeremiah 33:3, KJV)

There is something deep, mysterious, and powerful about prayer. Prayer changes things. Prayer changes God perhaps (see Exodus 32:11-14,KJV). Prayer definitely changes us! Jeremiah 33:3 is one of the greatest encouragements to pray found in the Scriptures. "Call upon me": there are no restrictions, nothing named that we should pray for or not, just the simple invitation to call upon God! This invitation to prayer is followed by a promise: "I will answer you." God is not hard-of-hearing; He always answers! Perhaps we may not be attuned to His answer and do not hear Him when he does! Then He expresses the nature of what He will do for us in response to our prayers: "…will show you great and mighty things which you do not know."

It is said that the great George Washington Carver (www.cbn.com/cbnnews /us/2010/ february/george-washington, Date Accessed February 8, 2013) prayed for God to teach him about the universe. God replied that the universe was much too vast for anyone to comprehend it all. Carver then prayed, "Well, teach me about the earth." God replied, "Pick on something your own size." Carver finally prayed, "Teach me about the peanut." God showed George Washington Carver more about the peanut than anyone had ever known before, or since! He developed more than 200 products from the tiny peanut! Great and mighty things that you do not know! Call on God!

FINDING BALANCE

So God created man in His own image, in the image of God created He him; male and female created He them. Genesis 1:27(KJV)

"And the Lord God formed man of the dust of the ground, and breathed into his nostrils the breath of life:" Genesis 2:7 (KJV)

What does it mean that we are created in God's "image"? Various ideas have been asserted over the centuries. Man is a spirit-being as God is Spirit. Man is capable of communion with God. Humans are able to have a relationship with God. There is truth in all of these ideas. In dynamic terms, to be "created in the image of God" means you are special! You are unique! This was not spoken of animals or plants, only of human beings. This thought – that God created me in His image and that I am very special to Him-- is the cure for poor self-esteem. It is the beginning of true identity, exploration, and achievement.

Alas, some are prone to ride that pendulum too far and "think of themselves more highly than they ought to think" (Romans 12:3, KJV). It is dangerous and destructive to "look only on our own things" (Philippians 2:4, KJV). The marvel of God's Word is that there is a corrective in the creation story. Genesis 2:7(KJV) says man was "formed out of the dust of the ground." Get the picture: God stoops down, scrapes up dust, spits in the dirt, and forms a man-like figure. He then breathes into him the breath of life and man comes alive! To balance our tendency to think more highly of ourselves than we should, we should recall that in reality we are nothing more than a walking, breathing mud ball!

Balance is the key! We are special, each and every one of us! We are made in the image of God! We are no more special than anyone else; we are all made in God's image. And lest we should self-exalt too much, we are reminded that we are dust. These truths enable unconditional positive regard for all others!

UNVEILED FACES

And we, who with unveiled faces all reflect the Lord's glory, are being transformed into His likeness with ever-increasing glory, which comes from the Lord, who is the Spirit.
2 Corinthians 3:18 (NIV)

This scripture from Corinthians reminds us of the Old Testament account of Moses meeting with God on Mount Sinai. It connects the story of a covenant given Moses on two stone tablets that he had prepared to receive God's law. Moses was allowed to see the glory of the Lord in all of His radiance during the encounter. The experience was so profound that the face of Moses luminesced after he came down from the mountain. His face glowed so brightly that he wore a veil so that the Israelites whom he led would not be fearful when he spoke to them.

We have a new covenant in the form of the New Testament and have been allowed to experience the glory of God made present through the Holy Spirit. We do not need a veil, however, God wants our radiance to serve as a testimony to the transforming power of His son, Jesus Christ. Second Corinthians 3:18 also reminds us that we are a work in progress. Imagine, if you will that you are slightly tarnished piece of silver. Each day the owner of the silver works diligently on the piece to remove unwanted discoloration and stain. He seeks to reveal the beautiful object he has envisioned for all to see. The analogy suggests that we are not in the final state of perfection, but are approaching God's ideal with each passing day. Daily Bible reading, meditation, and prayer are central in revealing His ever-increasing glory.

SPOKEN WORD (ONE)

Death and life are in the power of the tongue. Proverbs 18:21(KJV)

The word of God contains many types of messages for you and me. Among the types of messages are the Principles of God regarding how to live an effective life during our time here on earth. One of those principles is the power of the spoken word. The principle of the power of the spoken word involves several components, a few of which will be highlighted within the next four meditations/reflections.

The first component of the principle of the power of the spoken word involves each of us recognizing the power that is contained within the spoken word. In Genesis 1:1-31 (KJV) we learn that in the beginning God created the heaven and the earth. How? Then God said, "Let there be light: and there was light" (Genesis 1:3, KJV). In Psalm 33:1-9 (KJV) we learn that by the word of the Lord were the heavens made and that God spoke -- and it came to be. In Romans 4:17 (AMP) we learn that God "speaks of the nonexistent things that [He has foretold and promised] as if they [already] existed".

SELAH – pause and think about that!

SPOKEN WORD (TWO)

Death and life are in the power of the tongue. Proverbs 18:21 (KJV)

Another component of the principle of the power of the spoken word involves how individuals receive salvation and forgiveness from God. The Word of God tells us in Romans 10:9-10 (AMP) that "if you acknowledge and confess with your lips that Jesus is Lord and in your heart believe (adhere to, trust in, and rely on the truth) that God raised Him from the dead, you will be saved. For with the heart a person believes (adheres to, trusts in, and relies on Christ) and so is justified (declared righteous, acceptable to God), and with the mouth he confesses (declares openly and speaks out freely his faith) and confirms [his] salvation". Also, in First John 1:9 (AMP) we are told, "if we [freely] admit that we have sinned and confess our sins, He is faithful and just (true to His own nature and promises) and will forgive our sins [dismiss our lawlessness] and [continuously] cleanse us from all unrighteousness [everything, not in conformity to His will in purpose, thought, and action]".

The Word of God tells us in John 3:16 (AMP), "God so greatly loved and dearly prized the world that He [even] gave up His only begotten (unique) Son, so that whoever believes in (trusts in, clings to, relies on) Him shall not perish (come to destruction, be lost) but have eternal (everlasting) life." In John 17:3 (AMP) we gain insight into eternal life when we read "this is eternal life: [it means] to know (perceive, recognize, become acquainted with, and understand) You, the only true and real God, and [likewise] to know Him, Jesus [as the] Christ (the Anointed One, the Messiah), whom You have sent."

The power of the tongue to confess Jesus as Lord and receive salvation, forgiveness, and eternal life. To know and have a relationship with God – contained within the Word of God and reflected by the power of the spoken word.

SPOKEN WORD (THREE)

Death and life are in the power of the tongue. Proverbs 18:21 (KJV)

Another component of the principle of the power of the spoken word involves how words can be used to enhance life. Examples of how words can be used in a positive/constructive manner are as follows:

1. Proverbs 15:4 (AMP): A gentle tongue [with its healing power] is a tree of life.

2. Proverbs 16:23 (AMP): The mind of the wise instructs his mouth.

3. Ecclesiastes 5:6 (AMP): Do not allow your mouth to cause your body to sin.

4. Proverbs 18:4 (AMP): The words of a [discreet and wise] man's mouth are…[sparkling, fresh, pure, and life-giving].

5. Proverbs 17:24 (AMP): A man of understanding sets skillful and Godly wisdom before his face.

6. Proverbs 12:18 (AMP): The tongue of the wise brings healing.

7. Proverbs 11:11 (AMP): By the blessing of the influence of the upright and God's favor [because of them] the city is exalted.

8. Matthew 12:37(AMP): by your words you will be justified and acquitted.

9. Ephesians 5:4 (AMP): Let there be no filthiness (obscenity, indecency) nor foolish and sinful (silly and corrupt) talk, nor coarse jesting, which are not fitting or becoming; but instead voice your thankfulness [to God].

10. Second Peter 2:6-8 (AMP): and He (God) condemned to ruin and extinction the cities of Sodom and Gomorrah, reducing them to ashes [and thus] set them forth as an example to those who would be ungodly. And he (God) rescued righteous Lot, greatly worn out and distressed by the wanton ways of the ungodly and lawless – for that just man, living there among them tortured his righteous soul every day with what he saw and heard of their unlawful and wicked deeds.

11. Isaiah 50:4/Proverbs 15:23/ Second Timothy 4:2 (AMP)

Paraphrase: God teaches a Christian how to speak so as to bless and encourage others.

12. Deuteronomy 11:18-32 (AMP) Paraphrase: The word of God is to influence your daily life – what you think, say, and do.

13. Ephesians 4:29 (AMP): Let no foul or polluting language, nor evil word nor unwholesome or worthless talk [ever] come out of your mouth, but only such [speech] as is good and beneficial to the spiritual progress of others, as is fitting to the need and the occasion, that it may be a blessing and give grace (God's favor) to those who hear it.

14. Matthew 5:37 (AMP): Let your yes be simply yes, and your no be simply no.

15. Ephesians 4:15 (AMP): Let our lives lovingly express truth [in all things, speaking truly, dealing truly, living truly]

16. Psalm 39:1 (AMP): I will take heed and guard my ways, that I may sin not with my tongue; I will muzzle my mouth.

17. James 3:10 (NLT): Blessing and cursing come pouring out of the same mouth. Surely, my brothers and sisters, this is not right. The New International Version states that "this should not be."

Take time to monitor the words that come out of your mouth throughout the day. Are your words more in the category of those that enhance life, or are your words more in the category of "this should not be"? There is power in the spoken word!

SPOKEN WORD (FOUR)

Death and life are in the power of the tongue. Proverbs 18:21 (KJV)

Another component of the principle of the power of the spoken word involves how words can be used to destroy life. Examples of how words can be used in a negative/destructive manner are as follows:

1. Proverbs 15:2 (AMP): …The mouth of the [self confident] fool pours out folly.

2. Proverbs 16:28 (AMP): A perverse man sows strife.

3. Ecclesiastes 15:4 (AMP): …For God has no pleasure in fools (those who witlessly mock Him).

4. Proverbs 18:7 (AMP): A [self-confident] fool's mouth is his ruin.

5. Proverbs 17:20 (AMP): …he who has a willful and contrary tongue will fall into calamity.

6. Proverbs 12:13 (AMP): The wicked is (dangerously) snared by the transgression of lips.

7. Proverbs 11:11 (AMP): But [the city] is overthrown by the mouth of the wicked.

8. Matthew 12:37 (AMP): By your words you will be condemned and sentenced.

9. Proverbs 11:9 (AMP): With his mouth the godless man destroys his neighbor.

10. Proverbs 29:20 (AMP): Do you see a man who is hasty in his words? There is more hope for a [self-confident] fool than for him.

Take time to monitor the words that come out of your mouth throughout the day. Are your words more in the category of those that are negative and destructive, or are your words more in the category of those that would be considered positive/constructive? There is power in the spoken word!!!

ACCORDING TO THY WORD

"Be it unto me according to thy Word." Luke 1:38(KJV)

Never before in human history had such a thing happened! God had sent His messenger, an angel, to Mary to declare that she would miraculously conceive and bear a child, a son, who would be the Son of God! There was no history to compare; there was no paradigm for this! Mary's response was simple surrender; humble and total submission to whatever God was going to do: "Be it unto me according to Thy Word."

One can only imagine her questions, her doubtings, her disputations. After all, she was a virgin. She asked forthrightly, "How shall this be, seeing I know not a man?" (Luke 1:34, KJV). Every experience in all of human history made this an impossibility. The angel said, "For with God nothing shall be impossible" (Luke 1:37, KJV).

Has God called you to a seemingly impossible task? Are there insurmountable obstacles looming ahead of you? The Scripture encourages you to "Submit yourselves therefore to God" (James 4:7, KJV). God alone makes the impossible possible! Those who are proud and independent, feeling that they can handle anything by themselves, who sense no need for aid from others, much less God, are headed for disappointment and defeat: "God resists the proud" (James 4:6,KJV).

We can learn a great lesson from Mary. Humble submission to the will and purpose of God brings a channel of grace. Submission to God in faith makes the impossible possible!

FAITH IN THE FUTURE

Jesus saith unto her (Martha), Said I not unto thee, that, if thou wouldest believe, thou shouldest see the glory of God? John 11: 40 (KJV)

Their hopes had been crushed. Martha's brother was dead; he died four days before. Jesus, the only one who could have prevented the death, had not arrived in time. The despair runs deeply.

This is not an uncommon theme in our lives. The one we pledge our life to leaves for someone else. The child to whom we have given our best years, our greatest investments, turns a deaf ear and makes destructive choices that go against everything we have taught and held to. The company we have given our energies to for twenty years sells out, and our position is eliminated, and along with it, our income, retirement, and self-worth. All of the thoughts and emotions that accompany these experiences were with Martha at the grave of her brother, Lazarus.

Yet, Jesus says, I have already told you that if you would believe, you would see the glory of God! Can Martha actually believe that Jesus could salvage this tragedy? I am not sure if she believed that or not; nevertheless, Jesus spoke and Lazarus was raised from the dead, given food, and lived a considerable time afterward (John 11:43-44; 12:1, KJV). It was, indeed, a glorious event!

"Faith is substance of things hoped for, the evidence of things not seen" (Hebrews 11:1, KJV). Faith undergirds our hopes. Faith gives us the ability to set goals and pursue them. Faith supports our aspirations. Faith gives continuance to our visions. Faith is the "substance of things hoped for." Faith is "the evidence of things not seen." The very fact that we can envision a future is evidence that the future is possible! The application of creativity and imagination in our thinking about the future is evidence that it just may become our reality.

When hope is crushed, and expectations are disappointed, the way through is to believe in your vision of a changed future! If you cannot envision changed circumstances in your future, believe in the possibility of a changed YOU!

AGAPE LOVE

"For God so loved the world, that He gave His only begotten Son, that whosoever believeth in Him should not perish, but have everlasting life."   John 3:16(KJV)

The New Testament writers coined a special word to illustrate this unique kind of love. The word is "agape." This out-of-the-ordinary, God-kind of love is the sacrifice of self in order to meet the needs of another. Is this not what Jesus did? He said, "Greater love hath no man than this, that a man lay down his life for his friends" (John 15:13, KJV). That is exactly what Jesus did! All acts of love and devotion must be measured against this ultimate example. "Herein is love, not that we love God, but that He loved us, and sent His Son..." (I John 4:10, KJV).

Love is giving: "...that He gave..."

Love is indiscriminate: "...so loved the world..."

Love offers reclamation and redemption: that we "...should not perish..."

Genuine love for others is filled with these same characteristics. Love shows unconditional positive regard, unbiased, non-prejudicial, non-judgmental respect for all others. Genuine love invests self in the well-being of others. Genuine love offers a redemptive outcome; what an alternative to the self-destructive, "perishing" style of life! As one who is a helper to others, this is what you have to offer! Viva la difference!

FAITH EXPRESSED THROUGH LOVE

For in Christ Jesus neither circumcision nor uncircumcision has any value. The only thing that counts is faith expressing itself through love.   Galatians 5: 6 (NIV)

In this passage from Galatians, the Apostle Paul is teaching on the freedom that the follower of Christ should enjoy and how their freedom should be expressed. In the time this verse was written, the faithful were still having difficulty breaking free of the law requiring circumcision in order to be accepted into God's family. Paul is emphasizing that as Christians, we are no longer under the burden of the law. Rather, it is our faith expressed through love that marks us as disciples of Jesus.

We are instructed by Jesus that the sum of the law can be captured in two requirements. They are, "Love the Lord God with all your heart and with all your soul and with all your mind…; And the second one is like it: Love your neighbor as yourself" (Matthew 22: 37-39, NIV). The words sound simple enough, however, putting these words into practice is another matter. Take a close look at the world around you and it will become clear that love of this kind is in short supply. That is why Jesus charged us to set the example. Our faithful worship and our action-oriented display of brotherly love will set us apart and open the door for others to receive Christ.

Think about your behavior in these terms on a daily basis and put into practice what you profess to believe. After all, it is the only thing that counts.

DOING GOOD

…(Jesus) went about doing good… Acts 10:38 (KJV)

The ministry of Jesus involved both a supernatural and a natural component. Examples of the supernatural include:

A. John 2: 1-11(KJV) – Jesus changed water into wine;

B. Matthew 14: 13-21(KJV) – Jesus fed the five thousand;

C. John 9: 1-41(KJV) – Jesus healed the blind man.

Examples of the natural include:

A. John 4:1-42(KJV) – Jesus spoke with the Samaritan woman at the well;

B. Matthew 9:9-13(KJV) – Jesus ate with tax collectors and sinners;

C. Matthew 25:35-40(KJV) – The teaching of Jesus to feed the hungry, clothe the naked, visit the sick, and visit those in prison.

Each day as we go about our daily responsibilities, our path crosses paths with numerous people. The waitress at the restaurant, the cashier at the gas station, the mechanic at the auto repair shop, the person with the homeless/out of work sign on the side of the road, people who park in the same parking lots we do, etc. Each day we have the opportunity to show the love of God to someone simply by doing good to them.

Each of us can purposefully do good to individuals that we come into contact with daily, if we consciously choose to. A recent cultural phenomenon known as "pay it forward" or "random acts of kindness" provide numerous examples of going about doing good. Individually we must choose whether or not we will go about doing good. Hopefully you will choose to go about doing good, and if you do – we encourage you to be creative in how you can combine going about doing good with sharing the love of God.

Selah – pause and think about that.

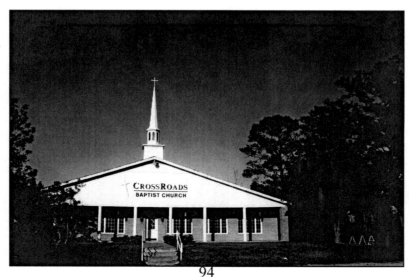

ROYAL AMBASSADORS

So we are Christ's ambassadors, God making His appeal as it were through us. We [as Christ's personal representatives] beg you for His sake to lay hold of the divine favor [now offered you] and be reconciled to God. II Corinthians 5:20 (AMP)

On Wednesday nights as a child, I was involved with a church program called Royal Ambassadors. The scripture, Second Corinthians 5:20, provided the basis for our name – and Wednesday night activities as a Royal Ambassador now provides cherished memories of yesteryear.

As Christians, we are all called to be Royal Ambassadors for Christ. We can serve as Royal Ambassadors for Christ by showing the Love of God through acts of kindness and acts of generosity to those we come in contact daily as each one of us goes about living our individual lives.

Think about the individuals you come in contact with (even if it is only momentarily) as you go about your daily activities. The shuttle driver who transports you from the airport parking lot to the airport terminal. The hotel clerk who checks you into the place where you will lay your head on a pillow for some sleep that night. The waiter/waitress in the restaurant who will bring you the food that you need. The person at the information desk who provides answers to questions regarding things you do not know. What I think, what I say, and what I do while interacting with these various individuals provide opportunities to share the Love of God through acts of kindness/generosity, IF I am willing to take just a little extra time while engaged in the interaction.

This meditation/reflection would have each individual do a self-evaluation regarding the use of time. Time is the great equalizer of life. Each individual receives a fresh batch of 24 hours each morning. The 24 hours can be used exclusively by the individual for self, or the individual can choose to include God as a partner in the 24 hours and act as a Royal Ambassador for Christ as he/she performs daily activities. Sharing the Love of God through acts of kindness/generosity while performing daily activities transforms you from being an ambassador of self, to being a Royal Ambassador of Christ. The scriptures command "you shall love your neighbor as [you do] yourself" (Romans 13:9, AMP). Loving others by being a Royal Ambassador for Christ is an excellent way to live out this command in daily life. Living as a Royal Ambassador for Christ enables us to fulfill the scripture, "Let us live and conduct ourselves honorably…" (Romans 13:13, AMP). Consider ways you can be a Royal Ambassador for Christ as part of your daily journey/ adventure.

GOD'S PLANS

For I know the plans I have for you, declares the Lord, plans to prosper you and not to harm you, plans to give you hope and a future. Jeremiah 29:11 (NIV)

God knows the plans He has for us! He sees the grand finale-- the end of a thing-- from the very beginning of it! We cannot. Some decisions…many decisions…maybe all decisions…must be made by faith….faith in an uncertain future made more certain by hope.

"Hope that is seen is not hope, for what a man seeth, why doth he yet hope for it? But if we hope for that which we see not, then do we with patience wait for it" (Romans 8:24-25, KJV). Ordinarily, the word "hope" is used for that which is merely wishful and uncertain: "I hope to live a long life and be healthy"; "I hope to go on a vacation next summer." Biblical "hope"-- Christian "hope"-- is not a doubtful or uncertain thing. It is the nature of the future God has guaranteed!

God does have a future for us! That is nice to know-- that we DO have a future! And even more, God has given us hope in the assurance that our future can be a prosperous one!

WORD OF GOD

For the word of God is living and active. Sharper than any double-edged sword, it penetrates even to dividing soul and spirit, joints and marrow; it judges the thoughts and attitudes of the heart. Hebrews 4:12 (NIV)

Sometimes we tend to think of the Bible as ancient history and not the living, breathing Word of God that it represents. Hebrews 4:12 makes it abundantly clear that God's presence is dynamic and very much involved in the lives of both believers and non-believers. There is no deed, motivation, or thought that can be hidden from Him who judges.

Let Hebrews 4:12 serve as your personal guidance system for making choices and decisions faced in life. The essence of this scripture reflects God's concern about the purity of motivation propelling the totality of our behavior, i.e., does the action lead to the glory of our Father in Heaven, or is it aimed at personal gain at the expense of someone else?

Is it frightening to you to know that God is aware of our thoughts and deeds that we keep as secrets? Instead of being paralyzed with fear -- or worse – acting out of intentional disobedience, use His Word to correct your thinking and bring it into line with God's expectations. Allow righteous thinking to guide your every action. This is the path to a peaceful and joyful life and full fellowship with Jesus Christ.

SEND ME

Then I heard the voice of the Lord saying, "Whom shall I send? And who will go with us?" And I said, "Here I am. Send me!" Isaiah 6:8 (NIV)

Beyond question, Isaiah was God's man for the job, a very unpleasant job at that. Most of us would be hesitant to accept the charge, yet Isaiah did not blink an eye. He just said, "Here I am. Send me!" You see, Isaiah placed His full trust and confidence in the Father knowing that whatever He needed to carry out the task would be provided.

God often calls us to do His work by speaking to our hearts about meeting the needs of others through our spiritual and material resources. Do you respond in the way that Isaiah did, or do you dismiss the call to His service? There are many times in the course of the Christian's daily walk that we hear the voice of God but fail to say, "Send me!" All too often we say, "No. Not now." The reasons are plentiful: we are too busy at the moment; we are in a hurry; someone else will come along and take care of things, and the list of excuses continues.

Become aware of God's voice and realize that He has selected you to do His work for a very good reason. Practice responding obediently to His call, no matter how inconvenient or impossible the task. Someone, somewhere will be richly blessed by your actions. God's timing is always perfect.

ENCOURAGE

David also said to Solomon His son, "Be strong and courageous, and do the work. Do not be afraid or discouraged for the Lord God, my God, is with you. He will not fail you or forsake you until all the work for the service of the temple of the Lord is finished."
1 Chronicles 28:20 (NIV)

How lovely it is to have someone encourage us when we are anxious and afraid of the concerns that are occupying the worry spot in our mind. Solomon had the enormous and exacting task of constructing a temple whose specifications were given by God Himself. Can you even begin to imagine the angst associated with building an edifice of that significance? Solomon's father, David, did not hesitate to attest to God's reliability in working with Solomon hand-in-hand to accomplish His mission.

It seems this scripture has three lessons for us within the text. First, we are to be encouragers if we claim to walk in the footsteps of Jesus. We are to be on the ready with an uplifting message of hope to all we meet and greet. Negativism abounds, so let us become the fragrance of God's presence.

David's words also tell us that whatever God expects us to do in His name will be accomplished -- even in our insecurity and perceived incompetence to deliver the request. God is trustworthy to equip us for any task that we undertake for Him. Perhaps, most important, God will not fail or forsake us until we have finished the work on earth that we have been placed here to achieve. Let us strive to take captive the fear and insecurity that the great deceiver uses to paralyze us and undermine the work to be done. Walk in confidence. God is alive, and His presence is eternal. He is with you.

THE ECONOMY AND GOD

But remember the Lord your God, for it is He who gives you the ability to produce wealth, and so confirms His covenant, which He swore to your forefathers, as it is today. Deuteronomy 8: 18 (NIV)

Do you spend precious time worrying about financial security? The media is full of doomsday messages on the state of the economy, the monetary crises on many continents, the dwindling worth and devaluation of the dollar, and the list goes on. It certainly appears we ought to worry if we believe our future is in the hands of the treasury department and banks of this great country. People everywhere are seeking out experts to advise them on the best strategies for averting the seemingly certain financial system's collapse.

God's promise to His people in Deuteronomy conveys an entirely different message; a message of faith and confidence that eclipses the world's message of pessimism. We are God's people because of the decision to follow Jesus. Our citizenship in His Kingdom ensures His promise is as valid today as it was when it given to the Israelites. There is a condition to receiving this promise, as with all of God's promises; we must walk in faith and not by sight. He honors the faithful and considers the act of faith in the believer as righteousness. He gave life and breath to you and will surely provide for your needs through His riches and glory.

THAT DAY

Though He slay me, yet will I trust in Him: Job 13:15 (KJV)

At some point in life, each individual becomes aware that he/she will one day die. When "that day" is 20-30-40-50 years in the future, the impact of "that day" is not fully comprehended. When "that day" becomes one month and/or one week from today---"that day" begins to impact our inner most comprehension, and our inner most being. What will be the words that our minds can focus on as we approach the last hours and minutes of life? Yet will I trust in Him (Job 13:15 KJV) are the words that the Holy Spirit brought to my mind in the hour of my need. [Note: While performing some home maintenance projects, I was involved in an accident that demanded a trip to the Emergency Room. Test results indicated serious internal bleeding that necessitated immediate hospitalization. At night, in a hospital bed, with doctors unsure as to how to stop the bleeding, and with time moving at a very slow pace--- I had time to pray and ask for restoration of health, but with the prayer emphasizing "Not my will, but thine be done" (Luke 22:42 KJV).] God answered by granting restoration of health, for which I am very grateful! However --- "Yet will I trust in Him" --- are the words that brought me courage (not fear), hope (not despair), and acceptance (not anxiety) in my hour of need!!! YET WILL I TRUST IN HIM: Selah, pause and think about those words.

DISCOURAGEMENT THREATENS

And the people murmured against Moses, saying what shall we drink?
Exodus 15:24(KJV)

Moses can speak to us about discouragement! He had led the children of Israel out of Egyptian bondage. He had brought them safely through the Red Sea on dry ground. The pursuing army of Pharoah had been overthrown in the sea. It seems that the children of Israel should have known by now that God and Moses could handle any water problems they might have! Some people are never satisfied. Moses went from being a hero to being a "zero" very quickly! He could have been quite reasonably discouraged, right?

Great victories are at times followed by sound defeats. Simon Peter went from a great confession that only God could have revealed to him (Matthew 16:17-23, KJV), to being in league with Satan! Noah went from the heights of saving his family through the flood, to being an outright embarrassment to his sons as he lay naked in a drunken stupor (Genesis 9:20-23, KJV). Moses went from the victory over the Egyptians at the Red Sea to a place where there was only bitter water to drink (Exodus 15:23, KJV). The inevitable ups and downs of life can cause us to become discouraged.

It is easy to become discouraged when we have problems with people. Gratitude is a scarce virtue. Sometimes the greatest services performed are quickly followed by mass forgetfulness. At this moment, the children of Israel completely forgot everything Moses had done for them. While we do not serve others for the sake of their appreciation, it is easy to become somewhat discouraged, perhaps disillusioned, when there is never a "Thank you."

How did Moses handle discouragement? How can we? These are some simple lessons to reflect upon: First, do not take criticism personally (Exodus 16:8, KJV). Secondly, do not attempt to retaliate, or take your frustrations out on other people. Third, take it to the Lord in prayer (Exodus 15:25, KJV). When Moses prayed about the difficulty, God showed him an answer!

MORE GRACE

But He giveth more grace. James 4:6(KJV)

God gives more grace. "Grace" has been defined in many ways --undeserved favor, God's riches at Christ's expense -- implying that the substitutionary death of Christ for our sins is the payment of the penalty for our sins, which in some sense frees God to show His benevolent favor to us. This is the essence of grace. God grants to us that which we do not deserve, and cannot gain without His loving favor.

This wonderful favor cannot be received, or seen, by those who do not have a sense of need. For example, the proud, who are full of themselves, and think that they have need of nothing that they cannot procure on their own, are not candidates for grace.

The opposite of this attitude is humility, a sense of great need. Do you feel that you have "arrived"? Can you handle whatever comes your way? As you have journeyed, have you come to the awareness that you do NOT have all the answers; that you do not even know all the questions yet! That you are NOT omnipotent. Then, my friend, YOU are a candidate for grace…more grace!

SERVANT OF GOD

I am your servant; …I love your commandments more than [resplendent] gold,…I esteem as right all, yes, all your precepts;…Psalm 119: 125-128 (AMP)

Individuals must decide for themselves the type of psychological and spiritual mindset that they will possess and utilize in their everyday living over the course of their life. In Psalm 119, individuals are encouraged to possess and utilize the psychological/spiritual mindset that they will be a servant of God and that they will love/value the word of God because they know that the "whole teaching [of the law] is light, and reproofs of discipline are the way of life" (Proverbs 6:23,AMP).

The psychological/spiritual mindset that enables individuals to begin each new day knowing that they are a servant of God, that they love God, and love the Word of God – allows individuals to depend upon God, and the Word of God to provide light regarding the way of life. Knowing this allows individuals to pray: With as much time as God will allow me to have to give to the Kingdom of God; With as much resource as God will allow me to have to give to the Kingdom of God; I want to do the will of God; I want to do what God created me to do.

ENERGY SOURCE

He gives strength to the weary and increases the power of the weak. Even youths grow tired and weary, and young men stumble and fall; but those who hope in the Lord will renew their strength. They will soar on wings like eagles; they will run and not grow weary, they will walk and not be faint. Isaiah 40: 29-31 (NIV)

We can see in this scripture reading from Isaiah that God serves as the source of energy and stamina to those who place their hope in Him. It paints a poetically beautiful picture comparing the imagery of a soaring eagle to the obedient follower of Christ. Like eagles, we are able to glide above and over the trials and troubles regardless of our circumstances. This is the result of placing a complete trust and hope in God to keep His promises and deliver us from the evil forces that desire to rob us of our energy and have us accept defeat.

Note that God does not tell us that our lives will be trouble-free, but He does assure us that we can have victory in the race through the hills and valleys of our daily experience in the arena of life. We also have a choice to believe His word or look at it with doubt and unbelief. God did not create a world inhabited by a species of puppets programmed for blind obedience. He seeks our love as a matter of personal choice. Just as we want our children to listen to our wise counsel because they love us and not solely out of fear, so God seeks our fellowship. Write God's word on your heart and trust His reliability.

TWO SPIRITS

We have not received the spirit of the world but the Spirit who is from God, that we may understand what God has freely given us. 1 Corinthians 2:12 (NIV)

From this passage of scripture we can see that two kinds of spirits are operating in the world; one is the worldly spirit that has a personal gratification focus, and the other is the Spirit of God which is grounded in love and giving. They are indeed contrasting forces that compete each day to influence every decision we make. The voice we listen to will determine whether we live in chaos and crisis or experience the peace and joy of living for Jesus.

One may ask, "How can I learn to effectively discriminate between the opposing forces?" While there are no quick solutions, there does seem to be one time-tested approach; renewing the heart by studying the word of God and engaging in a consistent prayer life. Get God's word deeply planted in your heart so that it becomes natural to weigh your decisions according to His will. Consistency in reading and prayer will not happen unless we choose to set a specific time and place to honor God in this manner.

All of us need to remember that we are a work in progress and fall short of the perfection our Father is seeking. We are made acceptable only through the blood of Christ but have a need to overcome the desires of the flesh daily. Get started on the path to consistently hearing and obeying the true Spirit through study, prayer, and meditation in the Word.

AVAILABLE TO ALL

For the grace of God (His unmerited favor and blessings) has come forward (appeared) for the deliverance from and the eternal salvation for all mankind.
Titus 2:11 (AMP)

In Ezekiel 33:11 (AMP) we learn that God has "no pleasure in the death of the wicked, but rather that the wicked turn from his way and live." In First Timothy 2:4 (AMP) we learn that God "wishes all men to be saved and [increasingly] to perceive and recognize and discern and know precisely and correctly the [divine] Truth." However, each individual must choose to accept or reject the grace of God for him/herself.

In Romans 10:9 (AMP) we learn, "if you acknowledge and confess with your lips that Jesus is Lord and in your heart believe (adhere to, trust in, and rely on the truth) that God raised Him from the dead, you will be saved". Although God has made salvation available to all, not all will choose to enter into a relationship with Him. The fool says in his heart, there is no God (Psalm 14:1, NIV), however, God so loved the world that He gave His one and only Son, that whoever believes in Him shall not perish but have eternal life (John 3:16, NIV). The word "whoever" makes the grace of God available to all individuals (to you) —-- you must decide (individually) to accept or reject the grace of God.

THE PHYSICAL BODY

Do you not know that your body is a temple of the Holy Spirit, who is in you, whom you have received from God? You are not your own; You were bought at a price. Therefore honor God with your body. 1 Corinthians 6:19, 20 (NIV)

Before Jesus was crucified, He told His disciples that He would always abide with them through the infilling of the Holy Spirit. In this passage of the New Testament, Paul is teaching the followers of Jesus that they too were recipients of the Holy Spirit. He specifically cautioned against contamination of the physical body through sexual immorality.

In the present age and time, our ethics and moral practices have taken on very broad interpretations and applications. Under the guise of loving our fellow humans, all kinds of abnormal behaviors and lifestyles have gained acceptability. While it is true that we are to love our neighbors, it is not required that we accept behavior that is forbidden by the Word of God. Crossing the line of sound moral behavior always leads to harmful personal consequences to us and to those who love us.

God's counsel is a reliable source of wisdom and truth for making life's decisions. Apply it daily in the choices you make.

WISDOM DEFINED

Let us hear the conclusion of the whole matter: Fear God, and keep His commandments: for this is the whole duty of man. Ecclesiastes 12:13 (KJV)

The book of Ecclesiastes (from chapter one, verse one through chapter twelve, verse fourteen) provides us Words of Wisdom from Solomon. While the entire book is filled with Wisdom, for the purpose of this meditation and reflection, this author would like to focus on five key points of Wisdom from Solomon. Those five key points are as follows:

1)   Ecclesiastes 1:13 (KJV) ... I gave my heart to seek and search out by wisdom concerning all things that are done ...

2)   Ecclesiastes 9:5 (KJV) ... the living know that they shall die...

3)   Ecclesiastes 12:7 (KJV) ... the spirit shall return unto God...

4)   Ecclesiastes 3:17 (KJV) ... God shall judge the righteous and the wicked...

5)   Ecclesiastes 12:14 (KJV) ... God shall bring every work into judgment.

After sharing the Wisdom that he had gained from God and the Living of Life, Solomon shares his conclusions. In Ecclesiastes 12:13(KJV) Solomon states "Let us hear the conclusion of the whole matter. Fear God, and keep His commandments; for this is the whole duty of man."

One of the best definitions of wisdom that this author has read in recent days is as follows: "The ability to see, into the future, the consequences of your choices in the present" (Andy Andrews, 2009, *The Noticer*, page 65). Aware that you will die, your spirit will return to God, and that the judgment of God awaits each individual – each person needs to make decisions on a daily basis that will produce the consequences (results) that they desire to be recorded within the story of their life (when the individual has said and done all that they can say and do here on earth). Each day of life, every daily decision you make – contributes to your life's story.

Yes, each day you write another page of your life's story by the decisions you make. As you meditate and reflect on your life's journey/adventure up to this moment in time – only you can determine the degree of satisfaction you experience regarding the consequences of your choices. One purpose of this book is to provide principles that will help navigate course corrections for those who are dissatisfied, and provide beacons of light for those who are satisfied, but in need of encouragement that will be spiritually affirming!

Selah – pause and think about that.

FEAR

So do not fear, for I am with you; do not be dismayed, for I am your God, I will strengthen you and help you; I will uphold you with My righteous right hand. Isaiah 41:10 (NIV)

It is ironic that fear drives much of our behavior considering the assurance of God's Holy protection that is given to us in this passage of Isaiah. We may not think that fear plays very much of a role in our lives, but if this is so, why are we bombarded with advertisements that pitch products that we need in order to be secure. For example, it is suggested that if we do not buy gold we will soon be in financial ruin; or if we fail to use the right beauty products-- others will not find us attractive. There are many other appeals based upon fear as a motivation to buy.

Fear creeps into other areas of our lives, as well. We frequently fail to establish relationships for fear of rejection. As creatures with fragile self-esteem, it is hard to take the risks involved in living a full and complete life. This same fear is often the underlying reason we fail to turn to God for salvation, or, if we are members of His family, to seek Him out when we have missed the mark. When we get immersed in reading the Word, we will see that God is always available to receive us. This is true even when we have committed a most egregious transgression. His arms are wide open when we come to Him in repentance.

With God as your Father, you can take on life with freedom and courage. Yes, times may be threatening and fear-inducing, but as God boldly declares, "I will uphold you with My righteous right hand."

MOTIVES DESIRES

You desire but do not have, so you kill. You covet but you cannot get what you want, so you quarrel and fight. You do not have because you do not ask God. When you ask, you do not receive, because you ask with wrong motives, that you may spend what you get on your pleasures. James 4:2 (NIV)

The early Christian leaders placed emphasis on the plain meaning of particular scriptures. If the plain meaning was not obvious, then one should look to the immediate context to shed light on the verse(s) in question. Then, one should also and always investigate how the verse(s) in question squared with the remainder of scripture or try to see how the verse ties in to the entire biblical context. The plain meaning of James 4:2 seems to be, "you do not have because you do not ask."

However, a couple of qualifiers may be found in the immediate and nearby context. The first has to do with one's motives and desires. Often, if we see or think of something we want, we go for it! We will even fuss, argue, quarrel, and even kill, in order to have what we want! This seems to illustrate the selfish grasp of egocentric humanity, with no reference to God or religion at all. Then, in the religious context, one may ask God in prayer for things – an apparent pious act-- but the motive for such things is selfish pleasure, so we do not receive.

Yet, "if any man lack wisdom, let him ask of God, who giveth to all men liberally, and it shall be given him" (James 1:5, KJV)! This promise from the nearby context implies that the humble person, aware of his/her own need for the wisdom that only God can supply, asks God for such, and God responds favorably!

Can it not be said, then, that the fulfilled life is one focused on the lasting qualities for the inner person, and not simply on things that bring only temporary gratification? Selah--- pause and think about that!

EACH NEW DAY

This is the day which the Lord has brought about; we will rejoice and be glad in it. Save now, we beseech you, O Lord; send now prosperity, O Lord we beseech you, and give to us success! Psalm 118:24&25 (AMP)

Each individual needs to receive each new day with rejoicing and gladness. Why? The Bible teaches that great is His faithfulness and that His loving kindness is new every morning (Lamentations 3:22-23, AMP). As Christians, we can ask God for success and prosperity so that we have the needed resources to help build the Kingdom of God here on earth. The churches pictured throughout this book, regardless of how simple or ornate the structure is, required resources to build. The individuals who came to know and love God built the church as a visible testimony to their surrounding neighbors that God dwells among them. The visible church building became the outreach center that allowed/allows the people of God to carry the love of God and the message of God to individuals within the community (state, nation, and other nations around the world) --- one person at a time. Yes, each of us needs to rejoice and be glad for each new day--- because none of us knows what success/prosperity/opportunity God will give to each of us that will enable us to help build the Kingdom of God during that twenty-four hour period!

BE CHRIST TO SOMEONE

Pure religion and undefiled before God and the Father is this, to visit the fatherless and widows in their affliction, and to keep himself unspotted from the world. James 1:27(KJV)

Pure religion, according to James, is not primarily evidenced by the kind of liturgy we employ when we are in a house of worship, although that is important. The prophet Micah urged us to consider, "Wherewith shall I come before the Lord, and bow myself before the high God? Shall I come before Him with burnt offerings, with calves of a year old? Will the Lord be pleased with thousands of rams, or with ten thousands of rivers of oil? Shall I give my firstborn for my transgression, the fruit of my body for the sin of my soul? He hath shewed thee, O man what is good; and what doth the Lord require of thee, but to do justly, and to love mercy, and to walk humbly with thy God?" (Micah 6:6-8, KJV) Pure religion is evidenced in Conduct and Character. James places a high value on caring for the helpless-- the widows and orphans in their troubles. James also places a high priority on keeping ourselves unspotted, unblemished, from the world. The purest expression of real religion is an outgrowth of our relationship with God, or knowing God. What do we know of God? What do we know God is? Jesus said God is most like a Father (Matthew 6:6, 8, 9, KJV). What would a loving Father do? A Father would care for the widows and orphans! Perhaps we are most like God when we care for the helpless, the hopeless. As nurse Florence Nightingale (http://www.c-we.com/acelumc/100926.html) cared for a dying soldier during the Crimean War, he looked up to her face and said, "You are Christ to me." Perhaps you, too, will be as Christ to someone as you give hope to the hopeless and care for the helpless.

GOD PERFORMING HIS WORD

The word of the Lord came to me: 'What do you see, Jeremiah?' 'I see the branch of an almond tree', I replied. The Lord said to me, 'You have seen correctly, for I am watching to see that My word is fulfilled.' Jeremiah 1:11-12 (NIV)

Apparently, Jeremiah saw an almond tree in blossom...full, beautiful white blooms. That was the sign that the tree was near to bearing fruit. What was the meaning? That God was "ready to perform His word." Fruit was about to be born! In the historical context of this scripture, God was going to send the Babylonians to defeat Israel and take them captive because of their failure to follow Him, just as He had said He would do. This is one of many clear examples of God's utter faithfulness to keep His promises.

In your journey, you can be assured that God will be utterly and completely faithful to do what He said He would do. He will keep His promises. One of His greatest promises is the promise of His presence with you: "And surely I am with you always, even to the end of the age" (Matthew 28:20, NIV). Believe this promise! Look around you! What do YOU see? Signs are everywhere, like the budding almond branch Jeremiah saw that God is with you, performing His word.

Shadrach, Meshach, and Abednego…our God whom we serve is able…He will deliver us…but if not,… Daniel 3:16-18 (KJV)

The whole story of Shadrach, Meshach, and Abednego can be found in chapters one through three of the book of Daniel. The focus of this meditation/ reflection is how they responded with faith in God when confronted with a difficult situation involving life and death circumstances, as well as their spiritual/psychological attitude of believing and confessing faith in God regardless of how the situation turned out.

One of the difficult challenges that we face in our spiritual/psychological walk with God is when we experience responses to prayer that were not what we were believing/confessing for. Shadrach, Meshach, and Abednego were confessing that God is able and that God will deliver them, however, --- they had already decided how they would respond if God (though able) chose not to deliver them (but if not, we will not). [Note: Try to imagine the spiritual/psychological challenges that Shadrach, Meshach, and Abednego experienced as they were bound and thrown into the "burning fiery furnace." Try to imagine the spiritual/psychological joy that they experienced when God "delivered His servants who believed in, trusted in, and relied on Him!" Daniel 3:28, AMP]

Each of us needs, mentally, to prepare for how we will respond if the answer to our prayer is not what we were believing God for. Will we allow that experience to diminish our love, our faith, and/or our relationship with God? To insure that we do not allow that type of experience to diminish our love, our faith, and/or our relationship with God, we need to develop the same mindset of Shadrach, Meshach, and Abednego. "But if not, we will not." If the answer to our prayer is not what we were believing/confessing for, we will not allow that experience to diminish our love for God, we will not allow that experience to diminish our faith in God, and we will not allow that experience to diminish our relationship with God. This is the kind of faith that can expect miracles, but that does not demand miracles.

If not, we will continue to demonstrate the love of God. If not, we will continue to utilize our faith in prayer. But if not, we will continue to grow/develop in our relationship with God. We will, because we know God. We may not understand the "why" of the "but if not" – but we know God, and knowing God through our "book of remembrance" (please review the meditation/reflection "Book of Remembrance") compels us to continue our journey/adventure here on earth. Perspective regarding "but if not" can be found in First Corinthians 13:12 (AMP) where we read, "For now we are looking in a mirror that gives only a dim (blurred) reflection [of reality as in a riddle or enigma], but then [when perfection comes] we shall see in reality and face to face! Now I know in part (imperfectly), but then I shall know and understand fully and clearly, even in the same manner as I have been fully and clearly known and understood [by God]."

Selah – pause and think about that.

MYSTERIES AND SECRETS

…To you it has been given to [come progressively to] know (to recognize and understand more strongly and clearly) the mysteries and secrets of the Kingdom of God, but for others they are in parables, so that, [though] looking, they may not see; and hearing, they may not comprehend. Luke 8:10 (AMP)

There will be times in life that circumstances and/or events will occur that exceed our ability to understand. We can pray for God to assist us in understanding, but if understanding is not granted – in faith we must move on with life.

An example that I would like to share involves the death of an individual who died (in my opinion) much too young!!! The grief was overwhelming, and the grief was compounded by not understanding why God would allow this to happen.

Understanding was prayed for, but understanding was not granted (at that point in time). In faith this author moved on with life, however, this author also experienced lingering faith questions similar to those that C. S. Lewis described in his 1961 book "A Grief Observed."

Over the next several years, I continued living life as a person, as a Christian (experiencing some faith questions), and as a professional counselor. An interesting occurrence on this aspect of the journey/adventure was being able to witness individuals who had spent years of their life loving God --- then abruptly change to a life of sin and treat with such evil the family and friends that they had once loved. This experience of being treated in such an evil manner by the ones they loved often resulted in family and friends making the comment that, "this is worse than death. The person we loved is dead, but someone who looks like the one we loved continually inflicts heartache and pain upon us."

After several years of praying for understanding, God answered through scripture. In Isaiah 57:1 (NLT) we read, "The righteous pass away, the godly often die before their time. No one seems to care or wonder why. No one seems to understand that God is protecting them from the evil to come." Based upon life experiences as a person, a Christian, and as a professional counselor I could see many interpretations of the words "evil to come" – two of which I would like to share. The first involves God protecting the person from evil that could be inflicted upon him/her (e.g. the story of Job). The second involves God protecting the person from him/herself (e.g. the repeated counseling stories of a person turning to sin and inflicting devastating evil on self and /or loved ones).

Answers to prayer often require waiting and patience. In this particular situation, what this author/counselor learned from clients who had to witness loved ones get caught up in sin, and then endure the infliction of evil/heartache from the one they loved – brought additional insight/clarity to the words of Isaiah 57:1. In John 14:26 (NIV) we read, "but the counselor, the Holy Spirit, whom the Father will send in My name, will teach you all things and remind you of everything I have said to you." When it is time, the Holy Spirit will teach you "the mysteries and secrets of the Kingdom of God" (Luke 8:10, AMP). If you have to wait for the Holy Spirit to teach you-- accept that part of the journey/adventure requires faith in God, a trusting relationship with God, and a life of obedience and submission to God. Faith, trust, obedience, and submission to God even when you do not understand. Faith, trust, obedience, and submission to God even when you are having to wait on God. Faith, trust, obedience, and submission to God even when you do understand.

Bottom line--- live a life that is characterized by faith, trust, obedience, and submission to God! Deciding to live a life that is characterized by faith, trust, obedience, and submission to God will bring awesome amazement to you as you travel the path of your journey/adventure. Including God, the Spiritual, and the Sacred as part of the journey/adventure of life brings perspective, balance, and the ability to embrace the mysteries and secrets of life.

WAIT ON GOD

God acts on behalf of those who wait for Him. Isaiah 64:4(NIV)

A normal life is characterized by a lot of waiting. It seems that a considerable amount of time is spent waiting to check out at a grocery store or a department store. Oh, the time that is spent waiting to see a doctor! Consider just how much time goes by while we are waiting to receive a phone call, email, or text message.

In the context of this encouragement for us to wait on God, Isaiah expressed other varied feelings, as well. He expressed his longing for God to act; it almost appears as desperation: "Oh that Thou would rend the heavens and come down!"(Isaiah 64:1, NIV) My paraphrase would express it like this: "Oh God! Rip the heavens open and come and do something down here!" Isaiah uses the image of a volcano erupting and the fiery lava flowing down to burn, consume, and boil, everything in its path. He recalls times in the past when God "came down" and did terrific things that were unexpected! Now he wants God to do it again. All the while, even in his desperation, Isaiah "waited" on God; he expected God to act, maybe today! If not today, then tomorrow, and if not tomorrow, then soon! God would act! He was waiting on just that. Think of all the times when you needed God to act on your behalf, but you had to wait. Just think of all the times when God unexpectedly "came down" and did something wonderful! When the "fullness of time" comes-- when the time is right-- God will come down and act in behalf of those who are waiting for Him to do so! Are you waiting with anticipation?

POWER IN WEAKNESS

But He said, "My grace is sufficient for you, for My power is made perfect in your weakness." 2 Corinthians 12: 9 (NIV)

The apostle Paul was struggling with a great affliction. So great, in fact, that he pleaded to the Lord to remove the "thorn" in his flesh three times. If we have lived any time on this earth, we have experienced our personal thorns – some imbedded deeply and painfully in our flesh and others, just agitating surface splinters.

In our human way of thinking, pain is simply pain, and we want it to go away. For both physical and emotional pain, a quick solution is what is most often sought and expressed through our prayers and petitions. During His last hours of earthly life, even Jesus fell on His face and prayed, "My Father, if it is possible, may this cup be taken from Me. Yet, not as I will, but as You will."(Matthew 26:39, NIV)

Now that we know the rest of the story, we can see the wonderful work of grace that was the result of Christ's sacrifice on the cross at Calvary. In that remarkable moment when Jesus said, "It is finished," (John 19:30, NIV), all of humanity was reconciled and beckoned to join God's family. When you face one of life's many agonizing trials, turn your focus to the way our Master prayed to the Father and readily yielded to His will. Experience His ever-present grace with trust and confidence.

HOLY SPIRIT INTERCEDES

So too the Holy Spirit comes to our aid and bears us up in our weakness; for we do not know what prayer to offer nor how to offer it worthily as we ought, but the Spirit Himself goes to meet our supplication and pleads in our behalf with unspeakable yearnings and groanings too deep for utterance. Romans 8:26 (AMP)

God intends for us to build our lives on the principles of scripture (Charles Stanley, 1985, How to Listen to God, page 148). One of the foundational principles of the Bible is prayer. In Luke 11:1 (KJV) we find the disciples saying "Lord, teach us to pray." Over the years, each of us has learned to pray through Sunday School/Church, personal Bible study, and/or reading books about prayer such as "With Christ in the School of Prayer" by Andrew Murray (1953). However we have learned to pray, there may come times in life when we are confused as to how to pray. If/when that happens, one of the biblical principles that provide us encouragement and hope is knowing that The Holy Spirit "pleads in our behalf" and that Jesus "intercedes for us" (Romans 8:26, 34; AMP). When confused or confronted with a life situation in which you can only say and/or think one word--- say/think the word "Jesus", and know that Jesus and The Holy Spirit are before God interceding for you.

GIFTS FROM HEAVEN

John...said, 'A man can receive nothing, except it be given him from heaven.'
John 3:27(KJV)

It is so easy-- and so tempting-- to take credit for things that happen. John the Baptist is pointing to Jesus Christ as God's gift. He told listeners, "Do not be confused; I am not the Christ. I am only a messenger announcing who He is. Do not follow me; follow Him. He must increase, while I decrease." (John 3:28-30 paraphrase). John is acknowledging that his ministry is a gift from God. It was given to him from heaven. You have been to church. You have learned many great and spiritual truths. You have been to school. You have sat at the feet of good and experienced teachers. You have sharpened your skills. You have developed insight, perhaps even wisdom. It becomes so easy to take credit, to feel deeply within that you are the reason things are as they are. Be reminded that no person can receive anything, unless it is given to them by God. After all, "every good and every perfect gift is from above, and comes down from the Father..." (James 1:17, KJV). Receive your gift; receive your calling....and give credit where credit is due!

STAYING THE COURSE

Let us fix our eyes on Jesus, the author and perfecter of our faith, who for the joy set before Him endured the cross, scorning its shame, and sat down at the right hand of the throne of God. Consider Him who endured such opposition from sinful men, so that you will not grow weary and loose heart. Hebrews 12: 2 -3 (NIV)

The path that the Christian must follow is narrow and often difficult. After all, we march to a different drummer. As the old hymn suggests, we are like "…Christian soldiers marching as to war with the cross of Jesus going on before…" (Baptist Hymnal, 1956, edited by Walter Hines Sims, Onward Christian Soldiers", by Sabine Baring Gould). As we look at the current state of the world in which we live, it seems our core values run contrary to contemporary society in every aspect. If you take a closer look, however, you will see that not much has really changed since the days that Jesus spent on our planet.

Jesus sets the example for staying the course. His life, from birth to death on the cross, was filled with chicanery, opposition, and just plain hatred. Scant few moments of His time were spent as the object of adoration by loyal followers. Instead, He was reviled for bringing truth and light – the gospel to all who would hear. Would we be as persistent in delivering the message under such hostile circumstances? Are we willing to face the certain rejection that will come from faithfully sharing our witness?

Seek God's strength and courage each day so that you will not grow weary and lose heart. Examine the past blessings that you have experienced and live with an expectation of greater rewards to follow as you complete His work.

For whoever finds me [wisdom] finds life and draws forth and obtains favor from the Lord. Proverbs 8:35 (AMP)

One of the purposes of this book is to provide insights regarding Biblical principles for living an effective life. In Proverbs 9:10(KJV) we are told, "the reverent and worshipful fear of the Lord is the beginning of wisdom". By linking the lead scripture and this commentary scripture together, we discover that the fear of the Lord is the beginning of wisdom – and that if we find wisdom, we will find life and favor from the Lord. However, there are many other positive effects in living a life governed by wisdom. A few examples of the positive effects of finding wisdom include the following:

1. Proverbs 4:6 (AMP) Wisdom will keep, defend, protect, and guard you.

2. Proverbs 4:8 (AMP) Wisdom will exalt, promote, and bring you honor.

3. Proverbs 9:11(AMP) Wisdom will increase the years of your life.

These scriptures indicate wisdom is a foundational principle that each individual needs to live an effective life. In addition to being told how to begin our quest for wisdom, the word of God also provides a promise of God regarding wisdom, "if any of you is deficient in wisdom, let him ask of the giving God [who gives] to everyone liberally and ungrudgingly, without reproaching or fault finding, and it will be given him" (James 1:5, AMP).

The quest for wisdom is part of the journey for individuals seeking the principles involved in living an effective life. The reverent fear of the Lord is the beginning of wisdom, and asking God for wisdom is the way to overcome any deficiency regarding wisdom. However, "Wisdom is too high for a fool" (Proverbs 24:7, NIV) because "the fool has said in his heart, there is no God" (Psalm 14:1, NASB) and "the fool speaks folly, his mind is busy with evil; he practices ungodliness and spreads error concerning the Lord; the hungry he leaves empty, from the thirsty he withholds water" (Isaiah 32:6, NIV).

Wisdom has been defined as "the ability to see, into the future, the consequences of your choices in the present" (Andy Andrews, 2009, *The Noticer*, page 65). Each individual must choose for him/her self to seek wisdom or seek foolishness. The authors pray that as you consider this choice in your journey, that the Holy Spirit will open your eyes and illuminate what you will receive or forfeit based upon your decision.

TEACH US TO PRAY (ONE)

…Lord, teach us to pray… Luke 11:1 (AMP)

The Word of God contains many types of messages for you and me. One of the types of messages involves the Principles of God regarding how to live an effective life during our time here on earth. One of those principles is the principle of prayer/faith. The principle of prayer/faith involves several components, a few of which will be highlighted within the next seven meditations /reflections.

While talking with individuals who have the desire to pray, but just do not know how, an often heard comment is – "I do not know what to say." In the book of Matthew, Jesus provides a model to help guide our thoughts and words as we learn to pray. Jesus teaches us to "Pray, therefore, like this: Our Father Who is in heaven, hallowed (kept holy) be Your name, Your kingdom come, Your will be done on earth as it is in heaven. Give us this day our daily bread. And forgive us our debts, as we also have forgiven (left, remitted, and let go of the debts, and have given up resentment against) our debtors. And lead (bring) us not into temptation, but deliver us from the evil one. For Yours is the kingdom and the power, and the glory forever. Amen." (Matthew 6:9-13, AMP)

Learning the words of what is referred to as the Lord's Prayer will help guide our personal thoughts and words as we learn to pray. As Rick Warren states, "obedience unlocks understanding" (2012, What On Earth Am I Here For, page 74). As we obey Jesus in using the words of the Lord's Prayer to guide in learning how to pray, we learn, "prayer is speaking with God" (Neil Wilson [editor], 2000, The Handbook of Bible Application, page 471). Speaking with God about the everyday joys and challenges of our lives, and then listening to what God has to say in response—that represents the type of Prayer God desires. In Jeremiah 33:3 (KJV) we read that God says, "call unto Me, and I will answer thee, and shew thee great and mighty things, which thou knowest not." As Charles Stanley states, "God desires to communicate with us" (2012, The Ultimate Conversation: Talking With God Through Prayer, page 3). Effective communication requires both speaking and listening. Learning to pray effectively will require wisdom in both speaking and listening.

TEACH US TO PRAY (TWO)

…Lord, teach us to pray… Luke 11:1 (AMP)

When I was in private counseling practice, there were two common themes that came through the office door with Christian clients:

1) The person was in severe crisis; and 2) the person knew the scripture about praying and God would do what you ask (John 15:7, KJV; Mark 11:25, KJV; Matthew 21:2, KJV; Luke 11:8, AMP). The individual was praying for God to solve this specific crisis in this specific way. However, the individual was not aware of other key words that accompanied the words about praying and God would do what you ask. The other key words that were out of awareness or purposefully ignored are as follows:

A) John 15:7 (KJV) …if ye abide in ME, and My words abide in you…

B) Mark 11:25 (KJV)…forgive, if ye have aught against any…

C) Matthew 21:2 (KJV)…if ye have faith, and doubt not…

D) Luke 11:8 (AMP)…shameless persistence and insistence…

The words in the book of John tell us that, "if you live in Me [abide vitally united to Me] and My words remain in you and continue to live in your hearts, ask whatever you will, and it shall be done for you (John 15:7, AMP). The words "ask and it shall be done for you" are connected to the words "abide, forgive, faith and persistence." The words abide, forgive, faith, and persistence causes each individual to stop and reflect on the following:

1) What is my level of abiding in the Word of God?

2) Am I willing to forgive those who hurt me?

3) Do I possess faith the size of a mustard seed?

4) Am I persistent in my total relationship with God?

These are questions that all Christians (regardless if we are experiencing crisis or not) need to meditate/ reflect upon periodically throughout the journey/adventure. These questions can be helpful to not only individuals in crisis, but also by individuals seeking Spiritual growth and/or to enhance his/her personal relationship with God.

The principle of prayer being highlighted in this mediation/reflection is seeking to connect what we ask for in prayer to the words abide, forgive, faith, and persistence. To abide in the Word of God, to forgive others, to have faith the size of a mustard seed, and to be persistent in our relationship with God – are all part of the Wisdom of God regarding prayer.

TEACH US TO PRAY (THREE)

…Lord, teach us to pray… Luke 11:1 (AMP)

Another component of the principle of prayer/faith involves understanding the word "prayer". Prayer is defined as a "form of worship"; and as "an earnest or humble request" (Thorndike-Barnhart High School Dictionary, fifth edition, 1968, E. L. Thorndike and C.L. Barnhart). A request can be granted, but a request can also be denied/refused. C. S. Lewis provides words of wisdom regarding prayer when he states "All prayers are heard, though not all prayers are granted" (1947, Miracles, page 294).

In Matthew 6:10 (AMP) we are taught to pray "Your Will be done on earth as in it is in heaven." In the Garden of Gethsemane, as Jesus is about to be arrested/crucified, the words that He prayed were "Abba, Father, all things are possible unto Thee; take away this cup from Me: nevertheless not what I will, but what Thou wilt" (Mark 14:36, KJV). Jesus makes His request, "take away this cup from Me", but submits His request to the Will of the Father – "not what I will, but what Thou wilt." Each individual who prays a specific prayer request is making his/her will known regarding the request-- but the individual also needs to be able to submit his/her will to the Will of God.

The individual who understands prayer realizes that he/she is making a request – not a demand. The individual who is in relationship with God, who loves God – lives a life that is submitted to God (James 4:7, KJV). As the words of the old hymn "I surrender all" clearly proclaims, "I will ever love and trust Him, in His presence daily live" (Baptist Hymnal, 1956, edited by Walter Hines Sims, by Judson W. Van DeVenter). Daily love and trust Him requires submitting our will to the will of God. Daily love and trust Him, even if the prayer request is NOT granted. Daily love and trust Him, even when the prayer request is granted.

TEACH US TO PRAY (FOUR)

...Lord, teach us to pray... Luke 11:1 (AMP)

Another component of the principle of prayer/faith involves what you believe (what your true inner thoughts are in relation to God, Jesus, and the Holy Spirit), say, and do with the privilege of prayer, and the faith you possess. In this meditation -- reflection, we will spend time examining what the scriptures have to say about what you believe.

Hebrews 11:1 (AMP) defines faith as, "now faith is the assurance (the confirmation, the title deed) of the things [we] hope for, being the proof of things [we] do not see and the conviction of their reality [faith perceiving as real fact what is not revealed to the senses]." God's Word Translation (Hebrews 11:1, GW) defines faith as "assures us of things we expect, and convinces us of the existence of things we cannot see." Examples of faith reflected in what you believe are as follows:

1) Matthew 8:5-13 (AMP) A centurion came to Jesus asking for healing for his servant. Jesus responds to the request by saying, "it shall be done for you as you have believed" (verse 13).

2) Matthew 9:27-30 (KJV) Two blind men came to Jesus asking for healing. Jesus responds to their request by asking them "believe ye that I am able to do this" (verse 28), and then tells them "according to your faith be it unto you" (verse 29).

3) Mark 5:25-34 (KJV) The woman who came to Jesus for healing saying to herself, "if I may touch but His clothes, I shall be whole" (verse 28). When they were able to speak with each other about what had happened, Jesus shares with her that, "thy faith hath made thee whole" (verse 34).

It shall be done for you as you have believed, according to your faith be it unto you, and thy faith hath made the whole – requires each individual to meditate /reflect on what he/she believes, what are the words we speak in prayer, and what words are written in our personal book of remembrance (Please Review the Meditation/Reflection "Book of Remembrance"). The words, "They shall know [from personal experience] that I am the Lord their God" (Exodus 29:46, AMP) take on significant meaning when the person praying experiences answers consistent with the request.

TEACH US TO PRAY (FIVE)

…Lord, teach us to pray… Luke 11:1 (AMP)

In the current meditation/reflection, we will spend time examining the Principle of Prayer/ Faith in light of what you say. In Mark 11: 22-23(AMP) we learn, "have faith in God [constantly]. Truly I tell you, whoever says to this mountain, be lifted up and thrown into the sea and does not doubt at all in his heart but believes that what he says will take place, it will be done for him." In Luke 17:6 (AMP) we learn, "if you had faith (trust and confidence in God) even [so small] like a grain of a mustard seed, you could say to this mulberry tree, be pulled up by the roots, and be planted in the sea, and it would obey you." Say to the mountain, say to the tree – illustrations of the power of the spoken word (Please Review the Meditation/Reflection "Faith Mustard Seed") when our words of prayer are combined with the written Word of God.

In other meditations/reflections, we have already examined "the mountain" as major (big) challenges of life and "the tree" as "the smaller tasks of everyday living" – and that our relationship with God encompasses all aspects of our life, both big and small. That our individual mustard seed size faith in God can provide life-altering experiences as part of our journey/adventure, makes the spiritual (the sacred) REAL.

We need mustard seed size faith that can assist us in the small tasks of everyday living as well as the big challenges of life. However, what words should we say in prayer when our mustard seed faith has dwindled or disappeared due to difficult questions, confusion, doubts, and/or unbelief. The words of Mark 9:24, as found in various translations, provide excellent words for meditation/reflection when praying with faith that is diminished and/or challenged:

1. I do believe, help me overcome my unbelief! (NIV)

2. I have faith, make my feeble faith stronger. (BBE)

3. I believe, help my unbelief. (ESV)

4. I do have faith, but not enough. Help me have more! (GNT)

In the prior meditation/reflection, we examined the principle of prayer/faith in light of what you believe. In this mediation/reflection, we examined the principle of prayer/faith in light of what you say. In our next meditation and reflection, we will examine the principle of prayer/faith in light of some of the instructions that the scriptures provide to each of us regarding what we do.

TEACH US TO PRAY (SIX)

…Lord, teach us to pray… Luke 11:1 (AMP)

The focus for this meditation/reflection regarding the principle of prayer/faith involves examining some of the instructions that the scriptures provide to each individual regarding what to do. Some of the instructions are as follows:

1. Hebrews 4:16 (AMP) Let us then fearlessly and confidently and boldly draw near to the throne of grace (the throne of God's unmerited favor to us sinners), that we may receive mercy [for our failures] and find grace to help in good time for every need [appropriate help and well-timed help, coming just when we need it].

2. John 16:23 (AMP) …(The words spoken by Jesus) my Father will grant you whatever you ask in My Name…

3. First Thessalonians 5:17 (AMP) Be unceasing in prayer [praying perseveringly].

4. James 5:16 (AMP) confess to one another therefore your faults (your slips, your false steps, your offenses, your sins) and pray [also] for one another, that you may be healed and restored [to a spiritual tone of mind and heart]. The earnest (heartfelt, continued) prayer makes tremendous power available [dynamic in its working].

5. Philippians 4:6 (AMP) do not fret or have any anxiety about anything, but in every circumstance and in everything, by prayer and petition (definite requests), with thanksgiving, continue to make your wants known to God.

6. Colossians 4:2 (AMP) Be earnest and unwearied and steadfast in your prayer [life], being [both] alert and intent in [your praying] with thanksgiving.

7. James 4:2 (AMP) You do not have, because you do not ask.

In this mediation/reflection regarding the principle of prayer/faith, we learned some of the things that each individual is to do when engaged in utilizing prayer/faith. Come boldly, ask in the name of Jesus, pray perseveringly, pray for one another, pray in all circumstances, pray with thanksgiving, and that you need to ask.

Throughout the last three meditations/reflections, we have had the opportunity to examine the principle of prayer/faith in light of what you believe, say, and do. Meditating and reflecting on the principle of prayer/faith is critically needed in today's world because as has been pointed out by Andrew Murray "…the church and her ministers had, through unbelief, sloth, and disobedience, lost what was needed for overcoming the power of Satan…" (1953, With Christ in the School of Prayer, page 92). When Murray uses the word "ministers", he is not just speaking about professional clergy – he is referring to all Christians, because all Christians should be actively praying, submitting to, and helping fulfill "Thy kingdom come, Thy will be done in earth as it is in heaven" (Matthew 6:10, KJV).

The church exists in a world packed full of people who are hurting and who have a lot of needs. To effectively address the hurts and needs – Christians will need the wisdom of God and the resources of God that can only be obtained through prayer. The church (through the hands and feet of believers) could, one day, become the leading mechanism through which God addresses the hurts and needs of people on a much larger scale than exists today. However, to be able to assume that type of leadership role, the Christian community will need to learn to pray. As Andrew Murray has so eloquently stated, "…there is nothing that we so need to study and practice as the art of praying…" (1953, With Christ in the School of Prayer, page 8). Lord, teach us to pray!!!

TEACH US TO PRAY (SEVEN)

… Lord, teach us to pray…Luke 11:1 (AMP)

Throughout the last several meditations/reflections we have spent time with this principle of prayer/faith. There are many components of the principle of prayer/faith, a few of which have been examined in this introductory volume of Counseling and Spirituality- and additional components will be explored in future volumes. However, as a way of ending the principle of prayer/faith until some future time, this author would like to share some closing scriptures for meditation and reflections regarding prayer:

1.   John 15:7 (AMP) If you live in Me (abide vitally united to Me) and My words remain in you and continue to live in your hearts, ask whatever you will, and it shall be done for you

2.   Matthew 17:21 (AMP) …Except by prayer and fasting…

3.   Second Chronicles 7:14 (AMP) If My people, who are called by My name, shall humble themselves, pray, seek, crave, and require of necessity My face and turn from their wicked ways, then will I hear from heaven, forgive their sin, and heal their land

4.   Jeremiah 33:3 (AMP) Call to Me and I will answer you and show you great and mighty things, fenced in and hidden, which you do not know (do not distinguish and recognize, have knowledge of and understand).

5.   Matthew 9:38 (AMP) So pray to the Lord of the harvest to force out and thrust laborers into His harvest

6.   Matthew 5:44 (AMP) …Love your enemies and pray for those who persecute you

7.   Matthew 5:48 (AMP) You, therefore, must be perfect (growing into complete maturity of godliness in mind and character, having reached the proper height of virtue and integrity), as your heavenly Father is perfect.

These closing scriptures will hopefully serve to guide future meditations/reflections on prayer until we can resume examination of the components of the principle of prayer/faith. As we have already learned, "…There is nothing that we so need to study and practice as the art of praying…" (Andrew Murray, 1953, With Christ in the School of Prayer, page 8). Lord, teach us to pray!!!

THE WORD TO ACCOMPLISH

… so is My word that goes out from My mouth: It will not return to Me empty, but will accomplish what I desire and achieve the purpose for which I sent it. Isaiah 55:11 (NIV)

From the book of Isaiah, we have this beautiful, reassuring passage that God is in control of what was, what is, and what will be, i.e., the past, present, and future are regulated by our Father who is trustworthy in all matters. These words are echoed in many other places in the scriptures. For example, the Lord's Prayer given to us by Jesus instructs us to pray, "…Your Kingdom come, Your will be done on earth as it is in heaven" (Matthew 6:10.NIV). It is God's intent that we live in agreement with His word.

Can you even imagine what a wonderful place this world would be if everyone desired to love God and his neighbors – as we will in the place called heaven. Though we may not see it through our human senses, we are moving closer each day to the fulfillment of His plan of redemption for all who seek out and accept Jesus as Lord and Savior. So do not be disheartened. What your eyes see and ears hear represents input from the physical senses. Instead concentrate on believing the truth of the Word that comes to us from the spiritual realm. Finish the race with tenacity, courage, and the unwavering confidence that God is truly in control.

LOVE CASTS OUT FEAR

There is no fear in love; perfect love casts out fear.1John 4:18(KJV)

Human beings are said to have four basic emotions: happiness (cheerfulness, joy, etc.), sadness (melancholy, despair, etc.), anger (hostility, bitterness, etc.), and fear (terror, alarm, etc.) The Greek word translated "fear" in this passage is "phobos", from which is transliterated "phobia." Persons diagnosed with phobic disorders, generally, have paralyzing, debilitating, responses to an object or condition. For example, it is asserted that all human beings have four basic or underlying fears: heights (acrophobia), darkness (nyctophobia), snakes (heptaphobia), and spiders (arachnaphobia). Perhaps it is true; each of us has some varying degree of anxiety when faced with any of these things. Most of us learn to cope with these by staying away from the things that threaten us the most, i.e. we avoid high places; we stay out of "snakey" places, and so on.

There are other fears that we cannot as easily escape. We often fear the unknown. We fear losing ourselves, our identity, our worth, our personhood. We fear being used, abused, or taken advantage of. We fear "not being" (Paul Tillich, 1967, Systematic Theology, p 75). These fears cannot be escaped or avoided as easily as one can avoid a high place or the lair of snakes! These fears are psychological and spiritual and go with us everywhere. There is a cure, an antidote for such! "Perfect love casts out fear!" Perfect love is found in God ("God is love"- I John 4:16, KJV), and through God ("God dwelleth in us"------ First John 4:12,KJV). This love is knowable (First John 4:7, 8, 9,13, KJV). This love allows us and encourages us to find ourself, our highest and best self (I John 4:12, KJV). This love has entered our world and is available for us, to us, and in us (First John 4:9, 11, KJV). The all-powerful God of the universe has come to us, and His love is made perfect in us! This awareness has emboldened people of faith across the centuries (Hebrews 13:6, KJV; Psalm 27:1-3, KJV), and this experience of the presence and love of God can cast out your fears, as well!

133

THE ADVOCATE

And if any man sin, we have an advocate with the Father, Jesus Christ, the Righteous.
1 John 2:2 (KJV)

Advocacy is an important ethical mandate for counselors. The American Counseling Association (2005) Code of Ethics states: "When appropriate, counselors advocate... to examine potential barriers and obstacles that inhibit access and/or the growth and development of clients" (ACA Code of Ethics Section A.6.a). If you are encountering roadblocks to the achievement of your goals, particularly if others do not experience the same obstacles, it is encouraging to know that someone is working with and for you to remove those obstacles. This is a basic responsibility of counselors.

In the spiritual realm, Jesus Christ is the believer's advocate. Sin is the impediment to progress. Sin is the obstacle preventing abundant life. Sin is the barrier to spiritual and psychological freedom. In a manner too deep for mortal minds to plumb, Jesus Christ has worked and is working, to remove the barriers to freedom, to eliminate the impediments to progress, and to pave the way to abundant life. God is FOR you! Jesus Christ is FOR you! By His sacrificial death, Jesus has destroyed the enmity (Ephesians 2:15-16, KJV).

WITH AS MUCH

For David, after he had served God's will and purpose and counsel in his own generation, fell asleep...Acts 13:36 (AMP)

When we are born, each of us has a finite/limited amount of time to impact his/her generation for the Kingdom of God before departing planet earth. When meditating/ reflecting on the meaning/purpose of life, the authors would like to suggest that the following words become part of that process:

With as much time as God will allow me to have to give to the Kingdom of God;

With as much resource as God will allow me to have to give to the Kingdom of God;

I want to do the will of God;

I want to do what God created me to do.

In Matthew 6:33 (KJV) we are told "seek ye first the Kingdom of God, and His righteousness; and all these things will be added unto you." Our time and our resources are finite, but if our priority regarding finite time and finite resources is the will of God [not all about how I can use my time and my resources for what I want to do and what I want to have] – then God will provide the time and resources you need to fulfill your role in making "Thy Kingdom come, Thy will be done in earth, as it is heaven" (Matthew 6:10, KJV) a REALITY. Remember the words of John 15:5 (AMP) – "apart from Me [cut off from vital union with Me] you can do nothing."

Selah – pause and think about that.

AUTHENTIC GUILT

"If we confess our sins, He is faithful and just to forgive us our sins, and to cleanse us from all unrighteousness." I John 1:9 (KJV)

There are at least two kinds of guilt. Authentic guilt is the deep remorse of conscience, the grieving of the spirit, which results when one has violated one's own internal value system. We feel guilty because we are guilty. False guilt may be imposed on us from the outside. Others may accuse us of something that, in fact, we did not do, yet the accusation makes us feel a measure of guilt. On other occasions, friends or foes may remind us of our failures, and our sins. Upon mention of our failures, we feel guilt. Still further, our own memory may haunt us. The psalmist David said, "My sin is ever before me" (Psalm 51:3, KJV). I imagine that everywhere David looked he saw reminders of his double sins of murder and adultery, perhaps others. Each time he closed his eyes to sleep, his sins were pictured on the back of his eyelids. He could not escape.

There is a remedy for both. In the case of genuine guilt, confession brings forgiveness and absolution. What is confession? It is agreement with God as to the hideous, destructive, and damnable nature of our sins. It is an acknowledgement that we deserve nothing other than the deadly outcome of our sin. It is acceptance of personal responsibility. God's response?   He "is faithful and just to forgive us our sins, and to cleanse us…" (1 John 1:9, KJV). Genuine confession brings relief from genuine guilt.

False guilt, the kind imposed by others, manipulated by Satan, or resulting from our own memory, will be conquered by receiving and accepting God's promises. Once we have genuinely confessed our sins, we may then forever lay claim to God's promises, such as "Their sins and iniquities will I remember no more!" (Hebrews 10:17, KJV). The psalmist, who had been plagued with guilt, received God's forgiveness and rejoiced in his new-found freedom (Psalm 32:1-5, KJV).

Ask God to show you your own heart, to show you your sin, and allow you to see yourself as He sees you. Write down on a piece of paper all the things that He shows you, sins of act and thought, sins that you overtly commit, and the good things you have left undone. Name them; list them. Be specific. Agree with God about the nature of those things. Thank Him for His mercy. Burn the paper and the list of things on it, receiving God's forgiveness and His promise that He will never hold these things against you!

WHAT DO YOU WANT

And Jesus stopped and called them, and asked, what do you want Me to do for you? Matthew 20:32 (AMP)

As I write this morning, my wife and I have been experiencing a crisis. A minor crisis in comparison to some challenges in life, but something that was causing significant sadness/grief for the two of us for the past three days. We were praying individually and together regarding the situation, but it was getting more and more challenging to maintain faith/hope within each passing hour. Although I was praying and making my request known, I was also praying "not my will, but Thy will be done" – and please provide the grace and mercy for me to accept "Thy will".

Prayers regarding the situation had already been part of my morning activities, however, the first scripture that I read for the day was Mathew 20:32, "Jesus asked, what do you want me to do for you?". Logically my mind was saying "accept what is and make that part of your reality", where as my Spirit was saying "Jesus wants to know what He can do for me, so I need to in faith make my request". While there was a battle within me regarding accepting reality and keeping my faith/hope focused on an alternative reality – I believed that today was not the day to stop making my request. So I prayed with as much faith/hope that I possessed, and asked for forgiveness regarding my doubt and unbelief.

Shortly after speaking a specific request in prayer, what my wife and I had been praying and asking for over the last three days--- the prayer request was granted. Instantly, joy replaced sadness and grief. Faces that had been expressionless now reflected smiles. Eyes that had appeared glassy from tears when certain thoughts arose or certain words had to be spoken, now gleamed/sparkled because of happiness.

Today we rejoice because our prayer sustained us when the situation severely challenged the words of our prayer. We are also grateful to God for His grace and mercy that would have carried us through had the same situation ended differently. C.S. Lewis provides words of wisdom regarding prayer when he states, "All prayers are heard though not all prayers are granted" (1947, Miracles, page 294). On the occasions when our prayers are not granted, we pray for the grace and mercy of God to help us in accepting His Will. Today, however, our prayer was granted, and for that we are grateful!

CHILDREN OF GOD

So also, when we were children, we were in slavery under the principles of the world. But when the time had fully come, God sent His Son, born of a woman, born under the law, to redeem those under law, that we might receive the full rights of sons. Because you are sons, God sent the Spirit of His Son into our hearts, the Spirit who calls out, "Abba, Father." So you are no longer a slave, but a son; and since you are a son, God has made you also an heir. Galatians 4:3-7 (NIV)

From the first day you accepted Jesus Christ as your Lord and Savior, you became part of the family! Not only did you become an instant heir to all that God's Kingdom has to offer, but you were also gifted with the intimacy of His presence through the Holy Spirit. It is through the Spirit that we are privileged to have a constant open channel of communication with the Creator of the Universe. This, dear friend, is an awesome thought; that God loves us so much that He desires our presence in His throne room any time, and anywhere. He has established an open-door policy for all members of the family.

The question that comes to mind is how much do we use this heavenly access? Do you want to live in His will and serve others? Would you like to live a more full and complete life? It is all possible when we have daily conversations with God and follow His guidance.

BIND   FORBID   LOOSE   ALLOW

And I will give unto thee the keys of the Kingdom of Heaven; and whatsoever thou shalt bind on earth shall be bound in Heaven; and whatsoever thou shalt loose on earth shall be loosed in Heaven. Matthew 16:19 (KJV)

As Christians we are daily involved in spiritual warfare (Second Corinthians 10:3-4, KJV; Ephesians 6:10-18, KJV). C. S. Lewis states that we live in "enemy occupied territory" (1952, Mere Christianity, p. 46). In Matthew 16:19 Christians learn of a spiritual tool that each of us has been given to assist in this warfare. The spiritual tool involves binding and loosing, or what we choose to forbid and what we choose to allow.

Potential words of meditation/ reflection based upon Matthew 16:19 are as follows:

In the name of Jesus and by the power of the blood, I bind (forbid) all negative, counterproductive, and/or evil thoughts, words, actions that hinder God inspired thoughts, words, actions

AND

I loose (allow) the power of the Holy Spirit to enable me to have positive, productive, and/or good thoughts, words, actions that are God inspired thoughts, words, actions based upon the Word of God!

The question to consider at this moment in time is, "Which thoughts, words, actions will you forbid and/or allow in your life?". The war rages on day after day in enemy occupied territory and presents daily temptations/challenges to all individuals. Each new day, each new challenge – will require a response at that moment in time. What we have chosen to forbid and/or allow will be reflected in our response. By choosing to meditate on the Word of God, each of us learns to think like God would have us think, say what God would have us say, and do what God would have us do – thus influencing our response.

Individuals must choose for themselves which thoughts, words, and/or actions will be forbidden and/or allowed. The authors pray that as you consider this choice in your journey, that the Holy Spirit will open your eyes and illuminate what you will receive or forfeit based upon your decision.

THE ARMOR

Therefore put on the full armor of God, so that when the day of evil comes, you may be able to stand your ground, and after you have done everything, to stand. Stand firm then, with the belt of truth buckled around your waist, with the breastplate of righteousness in place, and with your feet fitted with the readiness of that comes from the gospel of peace. In addition to all this, take up the shield of faith, with which you can extinguish all the flaming arrows of the evil one. Take the helmet of salvation and the sword of the Spirit, which is the word of God. Ephesians 6: 13-17 (NIV)

It is easy to see from these verses from Ephesians that we are warriors who need to be fully equipped and never surrender to the enemy, Satan or his agents. In the pictures you have viewed of our military personnel in combat zones, they are armed and given every defensive and offensive piece of equipment they need to do battle. We need a different kind of armament that is much lighter and yet powerful in withstanding the worldly and spiritual attacks we are certain to face.

Note in the description of the heavenly armor that we are to wear, very little protection is available if our back is turned toward the enemy…a posture that suggests giving up and running away. The biblical instruction clearly indicates is that we must face the attack head-on. Fearlessness and preparedness go together. Stay in the word and get it deep-down within you - to the core of your spirit. Your daily prayer, Bible study, and meditation will serve you well and enable you to rely on His mighty power and stand firm with the confidence of victory.

FAITH MUSTARD SEED (ONE)

…If ye have faith as a grain of mustard seed, ye shall say unto this mountain, remove hence to yonder place, and it shall remove; Matthew 17:20 (KJV)

Faith like a mustard seed. A mustard seed is very tiny. Imagine a single grain of sand or the tip of a lead pencil, which is the size of a mustard seed. To satisfy your own curiosity regarding what a mustard seed looks like you can Google "Picture of a mustard seed." Bottom line, a small amount of faith in God can move a mountain. This author thinks of a "mountain" as some of the major challenges that each of us will have to face from time to time as we travel the path of our journey. Knowing that God is with us on our journey and that God will help us with the challenges that we encounter is a source of comfort and encouragement. Each person who is a Christian has received the promise from God, "I will never leave thee, nor forsake thee" (Hebrews 13:5, KJV). However, each of us must daily utilize our faith in God when challenges cross our path in the journey/adventure of life.

FAITH MUSTARD SEED (TWO)

…If ye had faith as a grain of mustard seed, ye might say unto this sycamine tree, be thou plucked up by the root, and be thou planted in the sea; and it should obey you. Luke 17:6 (KJV)

In today's American culture, things have become compartmentalized – with Christians tending to only turn to and/or seek God on Sunday, or when confronted with the "mountain" size events of life [e.g. September 11, 2001 – 9/11"]. However, in comparison to the size of a mountain – the size of a tree is significantly smaller. This author thinks of the "tree" mentioned in the scripture as representing hundreds of daily tasks that each of us performs as part of the journey of life (e.g. awaking to the alarm clock, dressing, driving, interacting with family, friends, coworkers, etc.), and that God wants to be part of our whole life – not just the few hours on Sunday compartment or when the "mountain" size events occur compartment.

The Word of God teaches that Christians should pray without ceasing (First Thessalonians 5:17, KJV), in His law doth he meditate day and night (Psalm 1:2, KJV), and on His law (the percepts, the instructions, the teachings of God) he habitually meditates (ponders and studies by day and by night" (Psalm 1:2, AMP). As Brother Lawrence taught through example, "… in his business in the kitchen (to which he had naturally a great aversion [Author's Note--- but that was his job in the monastery]), having accustomed himself to do everything there for the love of God, and with prayer, upon all occasions, for His grace to do his work well… by doing little things for the love of God" (1958, The Practice of the Presence of God, page18). Including the spiritual as part of the daily tasks of the journey of life is an excellent way of praying, meditating, and reflecting on the Bible – and may even lead to experiencing some of the adventure of life that is included within the mystery of God as the love of God is shared with others.

FAITH MUSTARD SEED (THREE)

…Mustard seed…Mountain
Matthew 17:20 (KJV)

…Mustard seed…Sycamine tree
Luke 17:6 (KJV)

…Lord, I believe; help thou mine unbelief
Mark 9:24 (KJV)

In the journey/adventure of life, there may come times that individually we become psychologically/spiritually overwhelmed. When overwhelmed our mustard seed faith may dwindle to the point that we are confused, plagued with questions, and/or filled with doubts. IF that should happen, OR, when it does happen – remember to pray the words, "help thou mine unbelief" (Mark 9:24, KJV). Those four words could be what your spirit needs to experience a resurgence of faith that enables you to develop the psychological/spiritual mindset, "This I will seek: to remain in the Lord's house all the days of my life in order to gaze at the Lord's beauty and to search for an answer in His temple" (Psalm 27:4, GWT).

FAITH MUSTARD SEED (FOUR)

...Mustard seed...Mountain...
Matthew 17:20 (KJV)

...Mustard seed...Sycamine tree...
Luke 17:6 (KJV)

...Lord, I believe, help thou mine unbelief...
Mark9:24 (KJV)

A meditation/reflection based upon the three scriptures above, is as follows:

I believe,

I believe,

I believe.

Lord, forgive my doubt and unbelief.

Help my faith to grow and develop into that mustard seed faith,

so that I can speak unto that mountain,

so that I can speak unto that tree,

and say be thou removed - and I would see it move.

That I would see the power of faith.

That I would see the power of prayer.

That I would see the power of the resurrection.

That I would see the power of God.

That I would see the power given to a Child of God (First John 3:1, AMP);

That I would see the power given to a Christian (Acts 11:26, KJV);

That I would see the power given to a Priest of God (First Peter 2:9, KJV)

To bring down the resources of heaven,

To help build the Kingdom of God here on earth.

As you experience the power of God, the power of the resurrection, the power of prayer, and the power of faith here on earth, and record experiences with GOD in your book of remembrance (Please Review the Meditation/Reflection " Book of Remembrance") --- your faith will grow in size from mustard seed, to golf ball, to baseball, etc. size faith --- so that God can work through you to help build the Kingdom of God here on earth. Faith the size of a mustard seed can accomplish much for the Kingdom of God!!!

SPIRITUAL BUCKET LIST

I have fought a good fight; I have finished my course... II Timothy 4:7 (KJV)

Nowadays we hear a lot about "bucket lists." This "bucket list" seems to be a list of activities a person desires to do while able, and before death comes. When friends talk about visiting beautiful places, doing adventuresome things, eating at notable restaurants, listeners are often overheard to say, "That's on my bucket list." Most of these things are matters of personal pleasure and self-indulgence. While there is perhaps nothing inherently wrong or sinful with such things, could it be that we should have higher priorities?

Do you have a spiritual bucket list? Can you make a list of spiritual priorities that you think the Lord would have you accomplish before you leave this world? The apostle Paul said, "I have finished the race..." Evidently, he felt he had accomplished his purpose(s) in this world. In another place, it may have been Paul who had said, "...let us lay aside every weight, and the sin which doth so easily beset us, and let us run with patience the race that is set before us"(Hebrews 12:1, KJV). Can you identify an internal compulsion that says, "You must do this before you die?"

Paul's phrases "run the race, fought the fight, finished the course" all imply that he faithfully persevered. He kept on. He pressed on. He stayed at the task. He "stayed with it"; he "stood by the stuff". Other similar phrases and sayings encourage you to faithfully persevere until you have accomplished your own spiritual "bucket list."

IMAGINE

…overcome (master) evil with good. Romans 12:21 (AMP)

Imagine a world in which the American Christian community produced a major daily newspaper that was circulated throughout the entire nation which people could turn to for objective news reports. Imagine a world in which the American Christian community operated a major television network that provided entertainment programming that was not focused on the negative/evil aspects of life. Imagine a world in which "Holy-wood" (not Hollywood) provided the motion pictures that packed American theatres and that were in demand by other countries to play in their theatres around the world.

Imagine a world in which the Christians in every country were united and providing primary leadership in addressing major challenges such as:

1) Providing food for the hungry.

2) Providing medical care for the sick.

3) Providing for the needs of orphans.

4) Providing the type of care that would transform prisons from "human warehouses" into centers of hope.

5) Providing the types of activities needed to assist girls/women rescued from the sex slave trade industry, as well as the types of activities needed to shut down the sex slave trafficking industry.

In Matthew 25:40 (AMP) Jesus tells us, "in so far as you did it to one of the least [in the estimation of men] of these My brethren, you did it for Me." Sharing the Love of God by helping people with needs and sharing the Love of God with people who are hurting – we do it for them, we do it for Jesus!

Imagine a world in which the Christian community all over the planet provided significant leadership in print daily news, radio programming, television programming, producing motion pictures, feeding the hungry, providing medical care for the sick, caring for orphans, bringing hope to prisons, and ending sex slavery – that provided an alternative in the marketplace of ideas to what currently exists. The type of warfare required to overcome evil with good has been a warfare in which the American Christian community has refused to engage in over the last fifty to seventy-five years by sounding "retreat" rather than "charge" (in this author's opinion). However, what do you do when you want to retreat, but there is no place left to retreat to? As Edmund Burke (1729-1797) states, "when bad men combine, the good must associate; else they will fall one by one, and unpitied sacrifice in a contemptible struggle" (http://en.wikiquote.org/ wiki/edmund_burke, date accessed January 10, 2013). A modern language version of the quote is -- all that is necessary for the triumph of evil is that good men do nothing.

Andrew Murray teaches, "there is nothing that we so need to study and practice as the art of praying" (1953, With Christ in the School of Prayer, page 8). Proverbs 29:18 (KJV) tells us, "where there is no vision, the people perish." Perhaps the Christian community needs to be praying --- praying for a vision regarding how to minister to individuals who are hurting and in need. Perhaps the Christian community needs to be praying --- praying for spiritual leaders from all spiritual rankings (from general to private, and from private to general) who would be willing to function together to make the spiritual vision become reality. Perhaps the Christian community needs to be praying – praying for God to supply the resources (food, clothing, buildings, medical supplies, personnel etc.) needed to make the spiritual vision become a reality.

Imagine a world in which the words "overcome evil with good" was one of the guiding principles within the Christian community as it fulfilled significant leadership roles in all forms of modern media (print, radio, television, motion pictures, etc.), in feeding the hungry, taking care of the sick, caring for orphans, bringing hope to prisoners, and restoring freedom to sex slaves. Imagine a world in which the words "overcome evil with good" was being played out offensively rather than defensively.

Imagine a world in which the Christian community could be depended upon to provide major leadership in addressing problems of today (the modern media, the hungry, the sick, the orphans, the prisoners, the sex slaves) as well as the problems that will accompany tomorrow. In Second Peter 2:8 (ISV) we learn that Lot, "for as long as that righteous man lived among them, day after day he was being tortured in his righteous soul by what he saw and heard in their lawless actions." The Christian community must choose. Choose to willingly continue allowing righteous souls to suffer torture, or, choose to pray and respond to the words of the Christian hymn "Onward Christian Soldiers" (Baptist Hymnal, 1956, edited by Walter Hines Sims, Onward Christian Soldiers, by Sabine Baring-Gould) – "Onward Christian soldiers, marching as to war, with the cross of Jesus going on before…at the sign of triumph Satan's host doth flee…hell's foundations quiver at the shout of praise…like a mighty army moves the church of God…". Overcome evil with good! If not Christians, if not the Christian Community, and if not the Christian Church –then who???

Imagine the Christian community, supplied by God, leading the way in ministering the love of God by touching lives as portrayed in this meditation/reflection. With God, all things are possible (Matthew 19:26, KJV). Call unto me, and I will answer thee, and shew thee great and mighty things, which thou knowest not (Jeremiah 33:3, KJV). Take time to imagine! Take time to pray!! Take time to help make a New Reality in which the Christian Community is involved both offensively and defensively in overcoming evil with good!!!

PEACE HARMONY

…Let Him search for peace (harmony; undisturbedness from fears, agitating passions, and moral conflicts) and seek eagerly. [Do not merely desire peaceful relations with God, with your fellow men, and with yourself, but pursue, go after them!]. First Peter 3:11 (AMP)

This scripture teaches that each of us should search for and pursue peace. Search for and pursue peace – peace with God, peace with other people, and peace with self.

First Peter 3:11 brings out the meaning of peace through the use of the words harmony and not being disturbed by fears, agitating passions, and/or moral conflicts. Search for and pursue harmony – harmony with God, other people, and self. Search for and pursue a life that is characterized by living in harmony with God, other people, and self.

The Council for Accreditation of Counseling and Related Educational Programs (CACREP) defines "spirituality as a sense of relationship with or belief in a higher power or entity greater than oneself that involves a search for wholeness and harmony" (CACREP 2009 Standards, page 63, http://www.cacrep.org/doc/2009%20standards%20with%20cover.pdf , Date Accessed 1/25/2013). CACREP utilizes a search for harmony to define spirituality, and First Peter 3:11 encourages individuals to search for harmony as a way to live in peace with God, other people, and self.

Other scriptures that can help facilitate the understanding of this concept of peace/harmony are as follows:

1) Romans 5:1 (NRSV) Therefore, since we are justified by faith, we have peace with God through our Lord Jesus Christ.

2) Romans 12:18 (AMP) If possible, as far as it depends on you, live at peace with everyone.

3) John 14:27 (KJV) Peace I leave with you, my peace I give unto you; not as the world giveth, give I unto you. Let not your heart be troubled, neither let it be afraid.

4) Second Thessalonians 3:16 (AMP) Now may the Lord of peace Himself grant you His peace (the peace of His kingdom) at all times and in all ways [under all circumstances and conditions, whatever comes].

5) Romans 8:6 (KJV) … to be spiritually minded is life and peace.

6) John 16:33 (AMP) I have told you these things, so that in Me you may have [perfect] peace and confidence. In the world you have tribulation and trials and distress and frustration; but be of good cheer [take courage; be confident, certain, undaunted]! For I have overcome the world. [I have deprived it of power to harm you and have conquered it for you.]

7) Philippians 4:6-7 (NRSV) Do not worry about anything, but in everything by prayer and supplication with thanksgiving let your request be made known to God. And the peace of God, which surpasses all understanding, will guard your hearts and your minds in Christ Jesus.

An individual who can successfully live a life characterized by peace/harmony with God, others, and self would be viewed as possessing mental health by professional counselors. Scriptures provide guidance regarding how to search for and pursue peace/harmony through faith, prayer, and the power of the spirit. Based upon the preceding it becomes apparent that for clients who include spirituality as part of his/her life, the counseling process can be enhanced by uniting counseling with spirituality.

The scriptures in this mediation/reflection regarding peace/harmony, when wholistically viewed with other scriptural meditations/reflections discussed throughout this book, combine to provide principles by which to live an effective life. The individual's personal experience of the sacred serves as an influence on his/her beliefs, thoughts, feelings, words, choices, and behaviors as he/she go about daily living life. Uniting counseling with spirituality as the individual searches for answers to questions involving meaning, belonging, and the principles by which to live an effective life is a relatively new phenomenon within the counseling profession. Mary Burke (et al) points out, "Spirituality, religion, and the counseling profession have had an uneasy relationship at times…many counselor educators consider spirituality and religion to be important topics in the training of counselors, but they have not necessarily incorporated this belief into their course curricula…" (Mary Thomas Burke, Harold Hackney, Patricka Hudson, Judith Miranti, Gail A. Watts, and Lawrence Epp, 1999, Volume 77, Page 251/252, *Journal of Counseling and Development*). Uniting counseling with spirituality will require knowledge of the sacred writing as well as the principles for living an effective life that are contained within. By putting pen to paper, the authors are seeking to convey principles for living an effective life based upon their life experiences as persons, as Christians, and as Professional Counselors. As Andy Andrews has pointed out, "Experience is not the best teacher. Other people's experience is the best teacher" (*The Noticer*, 2009, page 9). The authors have combined words of scripture, words of hymns, and photographs of sacred symbols – with words of personal experience conveyed in meditations/reflections to assist the individual in his/her personal meditations/reflections. Through personal meditations/reflections, the individual will hopefully develop the beliefs, thoughts, feelings, words, choices, and behaviors that will become the spiritual and psychological principles that will enable him/her to make the journey and to experience the adventure of life – and to do so in such a way that the life lived can be perceived as an effective life. Thus the title, "Counseling and Spirituality: Christian Biblical Principles Within Daily Meditations/Reflections For The Journey/Adventure."

CONCLUSION

The time devoted to writing "Counseling and Spirituality: Christian Biblical Principles Within Daily Meditations/Reflections for the Journey/Adventure" has brought with it many spiritual and psychological benefits – the most notable being that of an increased awareness of a personal experience of the sacred. The many responsibilities of life can sometimes keep us from seeing God in so many of the little things of daily living. So while there were many reasons for writing Counseling and Spirituality – this unforeseen benefit serves only to remind us, "the list of things to do in life" can unintentionally impact our experience of the sacred, and diminish our relationship with God.

A primary reason for writing this book was to provide spiritual information for individuals who have a spiritual dimension to their life, who are interested in bringing about life changes, and who are interested in including spirituality as part of the change process. The meditations and reflections contained within this book have words of scripture, words of hymns, and photographs of sacred symbols that have been linked together by the words of the authors to facilitate the individual in his/her personal mediations/reflections. Through personal meditation/reflection the individual will develop beliefs, thoughts, feelings, words, choices, and behaviors that will become the spiritual/psychological principles that will guide him/her in the journey of life. These spiritual/psychological principles that the individual develops through choices, and that will guide the individual's life -- have the potential for both good and evil as well as positive and negative.

Some individuals involved in the psychological and/or spiritual change process may choose to seek the assistance of a professional counselor to act as a facilitator throughout the change process, while others may choose not to. Some individuals involved in the psychological and/or spiritual change process may choose to include spirituality as part of the change process, while others may choose not to. Either way, the professional counselor needs to respect the right of the individual to choose what he/she thinks is best for them.

Information contained within these pages was brought together as a way of assisting counselors, clients, and/or individuals actively engaged in the change process – who want to include spirituality (from a Christian perspective) as part of the change process. While the information contained within these pages is not an exhaustive listing of all the Christian Biblical Principles by which to live an effective life, this introductory volume does provide a good starting point.

Examining spirituality in light of counseling theory can become a rather complex undertaking for some professional counselors as well as other mental health professionals because of certain realities that accompany the world of counseling theory. Within the world of counseling theory, there are over 400 counseling theories to choose from. Choosing a counseling theory is challenging, but choosing a counseling theory that will allow for the inclusion of spirituality presents an even greater challenge.

As part of my career in counseling, I have been blessed to receive licensure as a Licensed Professional Counselor (LPC) and as a Licensed Marriage/Family Therapist (LMFT). Multimodal Therapy (MMT, developed by Dr. Arnold Lazarus) serves as my theoretical guide when working with clients and/or teaching students who are learning to become professional counselors. One of the factors that contributed to the selection of MMT as my theoretical guide in working with clients was the ease with which spirituality could be included or excluded from the counseling process based upon the client's inclusion or exclusion of spirituality as part of his/her life choices. If spirituality was included as part of the client's choice of lifestyle, then spirituality became part of the counseling process. If spirituality was excluded as part of the client's choice of lifestyle, then spirituality did not become part of the counseling process.

The "BASICID" serves as the cornerstone of Multimodal Therapy. What each letter of the "BASICID" stands for is as follows: B – behavior, A – affect, S – sensation, I – imagery, C – cognition, I – interpersonal, and D – drug related as well as biological issues (Arnold Lazarus, 1981, The Practice of Multimodal Therapy, page 9). The counselor utilizes the BASICID to assess the client's concerns and then develop a comprehensive treatment plan.

If the client has a spiritual dimension to his/her life, then an "S" can be added to the BASICID, making it into the "BASICIDS"" – and including the "S" as part of the assessment process and the development of the treatment plan. With clients who do not have a spiritual dimension to his/her life, then the "BASICID" remains just the "BASICID". (Note: Those who would like to explore Multimodal Therapy with the inclusion of spirituality, please read "Spirituality and Multimodal Therapy: A Practical Approach To Incorporating Spirituality In Counseling", Russell Curtis and Keith Davis, 1999, Counseling and Values, Volume 43-N3, Pages 199-210, April 1999).

In the past, the authors have had the opportunity to write about and have published articles concerning sexual counseling and spirituality from several different approaches to spirituality. A listing of those articles is as follows:

1) "Uniting Spirituality and Sexual Counseling: Christian Tradition". 2004, The Family Journal: Counseling And Therapy For Couples And Families, 12(4), 419-422.

2) "Uniting Spirituality and Sexual Counseling: Eastern Influence". 2006, The Family Journal: Counseling And Therapy For Couples And Families, 14(1), 81-84.

3. "Uniting Spirituality and Sexual Counseling: Semitic Tradition". 2007, The Family Journal: Counseling And Therapy For Couples And Families, 15(3), 294-297.

However, the authors believe that spiritual principles for living an effective life drawn from spiritual perspectives and sacred writing that are not the ones we utilize in our daily lives would be more comprehensively explored and explained in a written word format by someone who does utilize the spiritual perspective and sacred writings of that spiritual perspective in his/her daily life.

The authors have written about counseling and spirituality from a Christian perspective regarding principles of God that can assist the individual in living a more effective life by allowing spirituality to influence thinking, saying, and/or doing. The authors encourage writer's with other spiritual perspectives to utilize the sacred writings of those spiritual perspectives to provide principles regarding how to live an effective life utilizing that specific approach to spirituality. Individuals with spiritual viewpoints that are not Christian are in need of assistance from their sacred writings regarding spiritual principles by which to live an effective life in much the same way as Christians are. Therefore, the authors look forward to reading the written works of others who are willing to share the spiritual principles drawn from other sacred writings regarding how to live an effective life based upon the spiritual perspective practiced by that writer.

The Council for Accreditation of Counseling and Related Educational Programs (CACREP) has included spirituality within the 2009 standards to ensure that graduate counseling students receive the training needed to practice as a professional counselor. The details regarding how to include spirituality as part of the Graduate Counseling Program are still unfolding, however, when viewed from the perspective of this author and his days as a graduate counseling student – the profession of counseling is light years ahead of where we were in the 1970's. The authors look forward to working with other counselors to map out "the details of how" to include spirituality as part of the graduate counseling training program.

For now, this part of our journey/adventure together must end. The authors believe that the words of the hymn "God Be With You" summarizes our prayer for you the reader as we approach our final meditation and reflection together, "God be with you till we meet again! By His counsels guide, uphold you…God be with you till we meet again! (Baptist Hymnal, 1956, Edited by Walter Hines Sims, by Jeremiah F. Rankin and William G. Tomer).

The words of Solomon serve as the final meditation/reflection for this book, as well as words of wisdom for those who know that life is a gift from God, and that entrance into the eternal draws near. In Ecclesiastes 12:13 (AMP) we read, "All has been heard; the end of the matter is: fear God [revere and worship Him, knowing that He is] and keep His commandments, for this is the whole of man [the full, original purpose of His creation, the object of God's providence, the root of character, the foundation of all happiness, the adjustment to all inharmonious circumstances and conditions under the sun] and the whole [duty] for every man." However, for those who not only know that the entrance into the eternal draws near – but have been blessed to capture a glimpse of the eternal, please take a few moments to meditate/reflect on those ending words of Solomon in conjunction with the closing words of. C. S. Lewis as he concludes The Chronicles of Narnia: The Last Battle (1956, pages 183-184):

> "There was a real railway accident," said Aslan softly. "Your father and mother and all of you are – as you used to call it in the Shadow Lands – dead. The term is over: the holidays have begun. The dream is ended: this is the morning."

And as he spoke He no longer looked to them like a lion; but the things that began to happen after that were so great and beautiful that I cannot write them. And for us this is the end of all stories, and we can most truly say that they all lived happily ever after. But for them it was only the beginning of the real story. All their life in this world and all their adventures in Narnia had only been the cover and the title page: now at last they were beginning Chapter One of the Great Story, which no one on earth has read: which goes on forever; in which every chapter is better than the one before.

153

EPILOGUE

I did not realize when I left my mother's home in Virginia on the afternoon of February 5, 2010 for a brief drive to the airport and a two-hour airplane flight that I was really driving into an exciting adventure with God. Upon arriving at the airport, I was informed of a weather front that was forcing the cancellation of a large number of flights. The decision to drive from Virginia to Alabama provided an unexpected twelve hours alone with God. Praying, Christian music, and Christian talk radio prompted a sermon outline, a massive deck of note cards, and ultimately the manuscript titled "Counseling and Spirituality: Christian Biblical Principles Within Daily Meditations/Reflections For The Journey/Adventure." The outline, that became the note cards, and that ultimately became this manuscript has functioned as my constant companion over the last three years. The last three years have been spiritually challenging as well as spiritually exciting. The words of James 4:15 (AMP), "If the Lord is willing, we shall live and we shall do this or that [thing]" have provided additional insight and understanding regarding the planning of the journey. Planning must also include or allow for the unexpected.

Trusting, obeying, and submitting our will and our plan to the will of God and the plan of God — well that adds true adventure to the journey of life. Trusting, obeying, and submitting to God allows God to take us to an alternative path — an alternative path that may just provide the blessing and favor of God that would have been forfeited had we forced our plan and our will to be the only alternative. A two-hour airplane trip, that became a twelve hour road trip, which became a three year research adventure — all because God showed up in weather. The Presence of God expressed in weather, expressed in changed travel plans, experienced through prayer, experienced through Christian music and Christian Talk Radio, and felt beside me in the passenger seat of a 1997 Ford Taurus Station Wagon--- transforming the journey into adventure. So the next time that unwanted and unexpected change comes into your life — look for God! God may just be waiting (if you can approach the situation with the right psychological and spiritual mindset) to reveal Himself to you, to make Himself real to you, and/or to do something special for you. That something may be as simple as transforming a negative experience into a positive experience — without really changing the experience, just changing your perception or attitude regarding the experience.

Cancellation of air travel that could have produced a large number of psychological and spiritual responses — and the choice I chose produced one of the most rewarding research/writing expeditions of my career. God showed up and turned a two-hour airplane trip into a three year research and writing adventure — an adventure that will continue to unfold for a least the next twelve to twenty-four months.

A threefold cord is not quickly broken (Ecclesiastes 4:12, AMP). Marvin Jenkins, Tommy Turner, and I have been blessed by God to work together on several projects over the years. Without friends and colleagues like Marvin and Tommy — this aspect of the journey/adventure would have been much more challenging. Walking this path of the journey/adventure together and witnessing the blessings of God in our past and our present, helps create bold anticipation for what God has yet waiting up ahead for us.

In Second Corinthians 4:13 (AMP) we read, "I have believed, and therefore have I spoken. We too believe, and therefore we speak." The authors have chosen to speak through the written word and share what our experiences have taught us about counseling and including Christian Biblical principles as part of the process for living an effective life.

We want to say thank you for taking time to read the words that have been written. If you would like to share with us your thoughts and/or reaction regarding this book, please write to:

Counseling and Spirituality, P O BOX 361, Jacksonville. AL 36265

Based upon availability of resources, we will respond as soon as possible.

Live long in health and prosper, even as your Spirit/Soul prospers.
3 John 1:2 (Paraphrase – KJV)

Jerry Kiser   Jacksonville, Alabama   February 24, 2013

REFERENCES

Counseling and Spirituality: Christian Biblical Principles within Daily Meditations/Reflections for the Journey/Adventure. Dr. Jerry Kiser, Dr. Tommy Turner, Dr. Marvin Jenkins

The Authors have exercised due diligence in referencing all articles, books, hymns, translations of the Bible, and World Wide Web information used in this book. However, should the reader discover any omissions or errors in any of the references, the authors would greatly appreciate notification of those facts. Notifications can be sent to: Counseling and Spirituality, P. O. Box 361, Jacksonville, Alabama 36265.

References: Articles

Curtis, Russell and Davis, Keith (1999)
Spirituality and Multimodal Therapy: A Practical Approach to Incorporating Spirituality in Counseling, Counseling and Values, Volume 43-N3, Pages 199-210, April 1999.

Turner, Tommy and Kiser, Jerry (2004)
Uniting Spirituality and Sexual Counseling: Christian Tradition, The Family Journal: Counseling and Therapy for Couples and Families, 12(4), 419-422.

Turner, Tommy and Kiser, Jerry (2006)
Uniting Spirituality and Sexual Counseling: Eastern Influence, The Family Journal: Counseling and Therapy for Couples and Families, 14(1), 81-84.

Turner, Tommy and Kiser, Jerry (2007)
Uniting Spirituality and Sexual Counseling: Semitic Tradition, The Family Journal: Counseling and Therapy for Couples and Families, 15(3), 294-297.

References: Books

Andrews, Andy (2009) The Noticer: Sometimes, All a Person Needs is a Little Perspective. Nashville, TN: Thomas Nelson, Inc.

Agnes, Michael E. [Editor] (2003) Webster's New World Dictionary. Cleveland, OH: Wiley Publishing, Inc.

Gladding, Samuel T. (1996)
Counseling: A Comprehensive Profession (Third Edition), Englewood Cliffs, N.J.: Merrill, An Imprint of Prentice-Hall, Inc.

Gold, Joshua M. (2010)
Counseling and Spirituality: Integrating Spiritual and Clinical Orientations. Upper Saddle River, N.J.: Merrill of Pearson Education, Inc.

Lawrence, Brother
Nicholas Herman of Lorraine (1611-1691)
First Published in the United States 1958.The Practice of the Presence of God, Fleming H. Revell Company.

Lazarus, Arnold (1981)
The Practice of Multimodal Therapy, New York, NY: McGraw-Hill Book Company

Lewis, C.S. (1947)
Miracles, New York, NY: Harper Collins Publishers

Lewis, C.S. (1952)
Mere Christianity, New York, NY: Harper Collins Publishers

Lewis, C.S. (2002)
Essay Collection: Faith, Christianity, and the Church (Edited by Lesley Walmsley). Hammersmith, London: Harper Collins Publishers

Meyer, Joyce (1995)
Battlefield of the Mind. New York, NY: Faith Words.

Meyer, Joyce (2012)
Change your Words, Change your Life. New York, NY: Faith Words.

Murray, Andrew (1953)
With Christ in the School of Prayer. Old Tappan, N.J.: Fleming H. Revell Company

Stanley, Charles (1985)
How to Listen to God. Nashville, TN: Thomas Nelson, Inc.

Stanley, Charles (2012)
The Ultimate Conversation: Talking with God Through Prayer. New York, NY: Howard Books

Tillich, Paul (1967)
Systematic Theology: Three Volumes in One. The University of Chicago Press, Chicago 60637.

Vine, W.E. (1940)
An Expository Dictionary of New Testament Words. Old Tappan, N.J.: Fleming H. Revell Company.

Warren, Rick (2012)
What on Earth am I Here for? Grand Rapids, MI: Zondervan.

Wilson, Neil S. [Editor] (2000)
The Handbook of Bible Application (Second Edition). Carol Stream, IL: Tyndale House Publishers, Inc.

References: Hymns

At the Cross
Isaac Watts and Ralph Hudson, Baptist Hymnal (1956), Edited by Walter Hines Sims

God be with You
Jeremiah F. Rankin and William G. Tomer, Baptist Hymnal (1956), Edited by Walter Hines Sims

How Firm a Foundation
John Ripdon Baptist Hymnal (1956), Edited by Walter Hines Sims

I Surrender All
Van DeVenter, Judson, W., Baptist Hymnal (1956), Edited by Walter Hines Sims

Onward Christian Soldiers
Sabine Baring Gould, Baptist Hymnal (1956), Edited by Walter Hines Sims

References: Translations of the Bible

(AMP) The Amplified Bible. Scripture quotations marked (AMP) are taken from the Amplified Bible, Copyright 1954, 1958, 1962, 1964, 1965, 1987 by the Lockman Foundation. All rights reserved. Used by permission.

(ESV) English Standard Version. Scripture quotations marked (ESV) are taken from the Holy Bible English Standard Version, Copyright 2001 by Crossway, a publishing ministry of Good News Publishers. Used by permission. All rights reserved.
(GW) God's Word. Scripture quotations marked (GW) are taken from God's Word, Copyright 1995 God's Word to the Nations. Used by permission of Baker Publishing Group.

(ISV) International Standard Version. Scripture quotations marked (ISV) are taken from the Holy Bible: International Standard Version, Copyright 1996-2013 by the ISU Foundation. All rights reserved internationally. Used by permission.

(KJV) King James Version. Scripture quotations marked (KJV) are taken from the Holy Bible, King James Version, Cambridge, 1769. (Public Domain)

References: World Wide Web (www)

www.authenticdiscipleship.org; Emmaus vs. Ministries of Silicon Valley, Contemplating God in Scripture. Date accessed November 10, 2012.

www.bartleby.com/236/86.html; Aurora Leigh by Elizabeth Barrett Browning. Date accessed February 21, 2013.

www.brainyquote.com/quotes/r/robertkenn/21273, Robert Kennedy, Date accessed February 8, 2013.

www.brainyquote.com/quotes/authors/j/jim_valvano.html, Date accessed February 8, 2013.

www.cacrep.org/doc/2009. CACREP Standards – 2009. Date accessed February 8, 2013.

www.cbn.com/cbnnews/us/2010/february/george-washington, George Washington Carver: Master Inventor, Artist by Charlene I. Israel, Date accessed February 8, 2013.

www.convenantnews.com/daveblack050816.htm; Moody's Thirst for God by David Black, Date accessed February 2, 2013.

www.c-we.com/adelumc/100926.html. Grow Up by Leslie Flynn. Date accessed February 8, 2013.

www.en.wikipedia.org/wiki/philip_james_elliot; Jim Elliot, Date accessed November 14, 2012.

www.marriagemissions.com, Cindy Wright of the Marriage Missions, Discerning the Difference Between the Conviction of the Holy Spirit and Condemnation of the Enemy. Date accessed November 14, 2012.

www.nytimes.com/1994/01/26/sports/super-bowl-xxviii-cowboy-offensive-line-sheds-annonymity-but-not-pounds.html, Super Bowl XXVIII; Cowboy Offensive Line Sheds Anonymity but not Pounds by Mike Freeman, Date accessed February 14, 2013.

www.nytimes.com/specials/baseball/bbo-reese-robinson.html; Standing Beside Jackie Robinson, Reese Helped Change Baseball by Ira Berkow, Date Accessed February 14, 2013.

www.thefreedictionary.com; Date accessed November 12, 2012.

www.womenshistory.about.com/library/etext/poem/blp_carney; Think Gently of the Erring by Julia Canney, Date accessed February 21, 2013.

www.youtube.com/watch?v=wj25a1_fyu; Carl Jung Video, Date accessed November 8, 2012.

http://en.wikiquote.org/wiki/edmund_burke, Date accessed January 10, 2013.

http://ethics.itt.edu/ecodes/node/4192. American Counseling Association (ACA) Code of Ethics (2005). Date accessed February 8, 2013.

Color prints of ***The Lamb, The Lion, and The Knight***,
can be obtained by contacting Creative Reflections.
Contact information is as follows:

Creative Reflections
P O Box 336
Choccolocco, Alabama 36254
www.CreativeReflections77.com

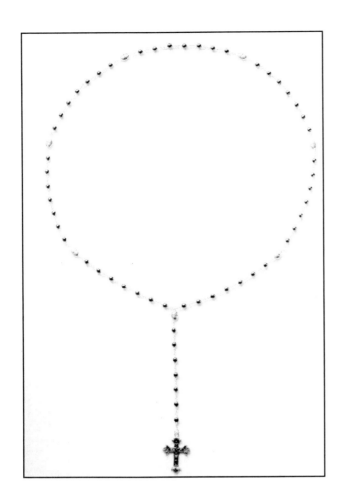
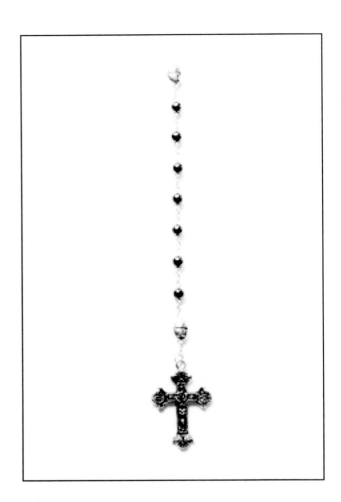

The C-MAPPER and/or C-MAPPER Companion Prayer Beads
can be obtained
by contacting Creative Reflections.
Contact information is as follows:

Creative Reflections
P O Box 336
Choccolocco, Alabama 36254
CreativeReflections@gmail.com
www.CreativeReflections77.com

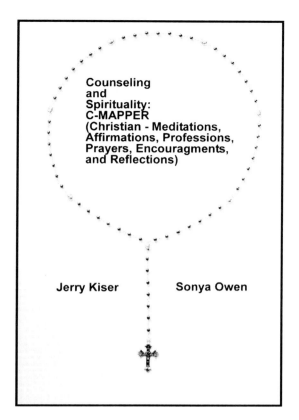

Counseling, Spirituality: C-MAPPER (Christian – Meditations, Affir-mations, Professions, Prayers, Encouragements, and Reflections) is a book that was created to compliment *Counseling and Spirituality: Christian Biblical Principles within Daily Meditations/Reflections for the Journey/Adventure* by facilitating focus through the use of something that is concrete/tangible in conjunction with the written/ spoken word. Copies of one or both books can be obtained by con-tacting Creative Reflections.

Contact information is as follows:

Creative Reflections

P O Box 336

Choccolocco, Alabama 36254

CreativeReflections@gmail.com

www.CreativeReflections77.com